Homeworld®

Prima's Official Strategy Guide

Rick Barba

PRIMA GAMES
A Division of Prima Communications, Inc.
3875 Atherton Road
Rocklin, California 95765
(916) 632-4400
www.primagames.com

ISBN: 7615-1576-3

Library of Congress Catalog Card Number: 98-65450

Printed in the United States of America

00 01 02 DD 10 9 8 7 6 5 4 3

CONTENTS

INTRODUCTION

Welcome to the official strategy guide for one of the most highly anticipated computer games in recent memory. When *Homeworld* made its public debut at the 1998 Electronic Entertainment Expo (better known as E3), jaws could be heard hitting the floor all across the Atlanta Convention Center. The following year in Los Angeles, E3 attendees voted a more finished version of *Homeworld* Best Strategy Game at the show. Anticipation grew downright sweaty and feverish as a multiplayer demo made the rounds in the summer of 1999.

Now the final version is in your hands. Blazing in full 3-D glory, *Homeworld* brings fresh perspective to its genre and clearly deserves to be tagged with that often-unearned term, "benchmark product." With an interface that makes 3-D movement of individual ships and massed fleets remarkably easy to master, the game is elegant and easy to learn. But conversely, like all great strategy games, it is equally hard to master. And that's where we come in.

HOW TO USE THIS BOOK

First, know that the informed sources of this book's content are indeed about as "informed" as you can get. Our thanks to Sierra's Quality Assurance team for providing detailed reports on each mission in the Single Player campaign as well as voluminous notes, tips, tactics, and strategies on how to beat the knickers off opponents in *Homeworld* multiplayer games.

Part 1: General and Multiplayer Strategies gives you exactly what it says. Chapter 1 starts with an in-depth look at the ships of the *Homeworld* fleet, then lays out general strategies for attacking, defending, and harvesting. Chapter 2 focuses on multiplayer action, offering advice on effective ways to develop and deploy your fleet against wily, unscrupulous human opponents.

Part 2: Single Player Missions guides you step by step through all 16 missions in *Homeworld*'s cunningly designed single-player campaign. Chapters 3 to 7 help you plot an efficient course from your first baby steps in low Kharak orbit to the doorstep of the Taiidan Emperor's Mothership hovering above Hiigara, your homeworld.

Good luck. Let this book be your own personal Guidestone.

PART I
GENERAL AND MULTIPLAYER STRATEGIES

People frequently ask me, "Do you really play all those games you write about?" My usual answer is no. I try to keep an open mind. I don't want "playing the game" to get in the way of developing effective strategies for the layman.

The truth, of course, is that I play each game until my eyes bleed. Still, if I had to concoct all the strategies and tactics for a deep game like *Homeworld* myself and still meet my deadlines, I might be several brains short of a good book.

Thus, I turn to my distinguished panel of experts, four guys who've played *Homeworld* morning, noon, and night through several disturbing election cycles. Nobody knows this game quite like Torsten Reinl, *Homeworld's* Quality Assurance Lead, and his team of testers. My special thanks go to Torsten and his awesome QA cohorts—Christopher Mason, Erinn Hamilton, and "Nautikus"—for their cogent and generous input.

Chapter 1
General Strategies

I open with some basic tips and tactics that apply to *Homeworld,* whether you play the single-player campaign or a multiplayer game. First, I define some standard group types for both offensive and defensive fleet maneuvers. Then I look at the strengths and weaknesses of each ship available in the game. Finally, I discuss general strategies for attacking and defending, and then take a special look at the unglamorous-but-essential activity of harvesting.

Group Type Definitions

The *Homeworld* testing team uses the following terms to designate certain types of fleet groupings.

Defense Group

This is the group of ships assigned to protect your Mothership (or, in Carrier-only multiplayer games, your Carrier).

Strike Group

This is a small, mobile group primarily comprising Strike craft—Fighters and Corvettes. Strike Groups usually harass enemy resource or research operations and conduct other miscellaneous quick-strike raiding activities.

Battle Group

This is the big Capital ship armada you slowly amass to take out the enemy's main group and Mothership. Battle Groups also include the various support and escort units necessary to conduct successful fleet-to-fleet combat.

Escort Group

The name says it all. This group is assigned to guard a particular ship or group of ships. Escorts usually guard high-priority but defenseless ships (such as Resource Collectors), or compensate for certain weaknesses of the guarded ship. For example, a group of Multigun Corvettes might escort a powerful Destroyer because of the big ship's vulnerability to Fighter swarms.

Capture Group

This sneaky squad is built around the Salvage Corvette, which can attach itself to enemy ships and "salvage"—that is, *steal*—them for you to use in your own fleet.

THE HOMEWORLD FLEET

We asked Sierra's *Homeworld* testers to evaluate frankly each ship in the fleet—strengths, weaknesses, and how best to use it. Here are their honest (and sometimes amusing) appraisals.

Fighter Class

Scout

Strengths

Quick, fast, cheap. And that's about it.

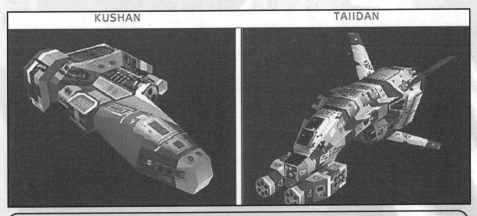

Fig. 1-1. Scout

Weaknesses

Weak armor. Low firepower, too—a measly 25. Overall, the weakest combat ship. "A kick in the shin will blow it up," says Torsten Reinl.

Using It Best

- Reinl: "Harass and annoy enemy harvesting operations."
- Nautikus: *Kamikaze!* Put 'em in Wall formation and slam 'em into your favorite enemy. Also good for general harassment and other suicide missions."
- Mason: "With the class-based unit cap for Fighters, about the only good time to build this unit is early in the game, before you've researched something better."
- Hamilton: "Raid enemy resource operations. Or deploy as an inexpensive counter to other Strike craft."

Interceptor
Strengths

Good balance of speed, firepower, armor and cost. Stronger than the Scout.

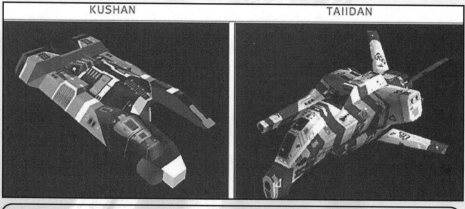

KUSHAN	TAIIDAN

Fig. 1-2. Interceptor

Weaknesses

"None really," says Chris Mason, "other than that it's a Strike Craft, which makes it less useful late in games when there are huge fleets of Capital ships flying around."

Using It Best

- Reinl: "Good all-around craft for attacking enemy Strike craft and harvesting operations."
- Mason: "Use in big groups of 20 or more in Claw or Sphere formation, primarily to raid or escort harvesters.
- Hamilton: "Same use as Scouts, only better."

Defender

Strengths

Gimballed guns give it excellent coverage of 90 percent. Also features good firepower. Nautikus calls it "the wrath of God in a small package."

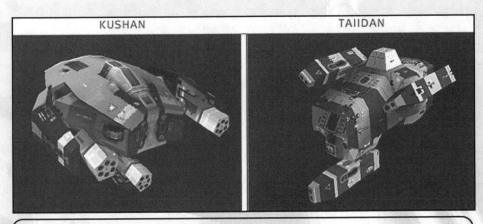

Fig. 1-3. Defender

Weaknesses

Fragile and very slow.

Using It Best

- Reinl: "Ambush and chew up anything dumb enough to show up without a Missile Destroyer."
- Nautikus: "Good for defending, but also excellent for taking out resource operations. I like them in a Wall formation."
- Mason: "Choose these over Interceptors when you don't foresee having to move them too far."
- Hamilton: "An all-around killing machine."

Cloaked Fighter (Kushan Only)

Strengths

Its cloaking ability, obviously. You can't see it coming without a Proximity Sensor.

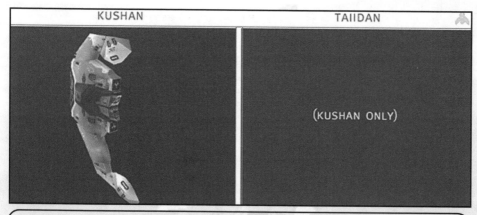

Fig. 1-4. Cloaked Fighter

Weaknesses

Expensive, with long construction times and low firepower. As Chris Mason points out, "For its high cost and *lo-o-o-ong* build times, it really isn't that great in combat. It's not like it can attack while cloaked."

Using It Best

- Hamilton: "Terrorism."
- Reinl: "Clandestine scouting and surprise attacks on high-value targets, such as a Grav Well Generator or Sensors Array."
- Mason: "Sneak attacks. It's just not good enough combat-wise to be a primary weapon. But when you want to launch a quick hit on a specific target (enemy harvester, Research Ship), these are your boys."

Attack Bomber

Strengths

Best firepower in Fighter class. Good weapon against large targets. Erinn Hamilton says, "The Taiidan one looks cool."

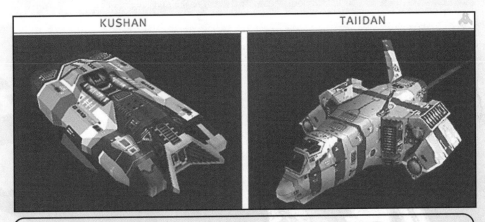

Fig. 1-5. Attack Bomber

Weaknesses

Very vulnerable to other Strike craft. Multigun Corvettes and Missile Destroyers can make mincemeat of Attack Bomber wings.

Using It Best

- Awesome against Frigates and Resource Collectors.
- Hamilton: "An Attack Bomber wing is best paired with an escort of Corvettes or Defenders—something to keep enemy Strike craft off its back."

Defense Fighter (Taiidan Only)

Strengths

Shoots down incoming fire. And it's kind of cute.

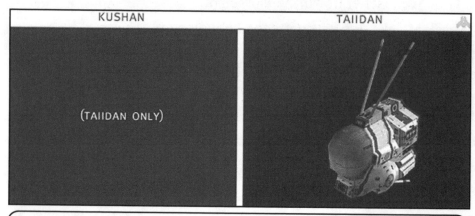

KUSHAN | TAIIDAN

(TAIIDAN ONLY)

Fig. 1-6. Defense Fighter

Weaknesses

No offensive capability whatsoever.

Using It Best

- Nautikus: "Put it in a Sphere guarding ships you care about."
- Mason: "Defense? Please. I'm way too aggressive for that."

Corvette Class

Light Corvette

Strengths

Decent firepower for small Strike craft. Relatively cheap and quick to make.

Weaknesses

Slow. Firepower pales in comparison to bigger craft. Chris Mason adds, "For the cost, I'd rather have the equivalent number of Interceptors."

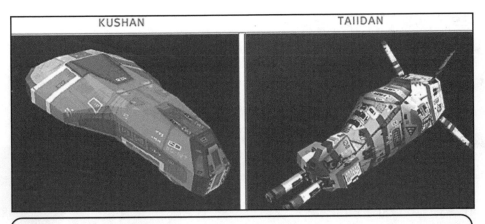

| KUSHAN | TAIIDAN |

Fig. 1-7. Light Corvette

Using It Best

- Reinl: "Popping Scouts and Interceptors."
- Hamilton: "As a raider."
- Mason: "Don't."

Heavy Corvette

Strengths

Good firepower in a small package. Multiple targeting—twin turrets lets it track two Fighters at once. Good armor, too.

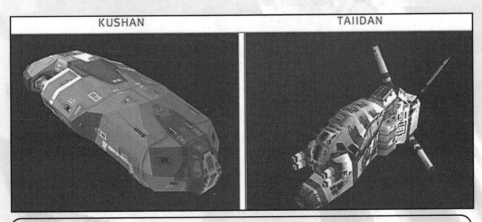

| KUSHAN | TAIIDAN |

Fig. 1-8. Heavy Corvette

Weaknesses

Slow and relatively expensive. Low rate of fire compared to other Strike craft.

Using It Best

- Reinl: "Attack other Strike craft and, with numbers, take on Ion Cannon Frigates."
- Mason: "Use groups of Heavy Corvettes in Claw formation to eliminate enemy Fighters—at least until you research to Multigun Corvettes."
- Hamilton: "Strike craft removal."

Repair Corvette
Strengths

Obviously, it can repair ships.

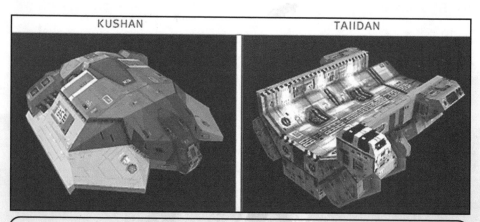

| KUSHAN | TAIIDAN |

Fig. 1-9. Repair Corvette

Weaknesses

No firepower; thin Strike craft armor. Torsten Reinl says, "Anything bigger can kill it with one or two shots."

Using It Best

- Reinl: "Repair *anything* that needs repairing. Try having a bunch of Repair Corvettes suck on your Mothership while it's being attacked."
- Nautikus: "I try to keep some with my Frigate groups."

- Hamilton: "Kamikaze."
- Mason: "Because Strike craft are repaired when they dock, and Capital ships can repair themselves (albeit slowly), I use these only in situations where I really need to repair damage more quickly than usual—if, say, the Mothership just got slammed and another enemy fleet is advancing. A good place for a Repair Corvette is Mission 10, 'Super Nova Research Station.' I send one with my fleet in case of too much radiation damage."

Salvage Corvette

Strengths

Can steal enemy ships. This is a favorite Torsten Reinl tactic. Chris Mason says, "This is *big*. Stealing enemy ships is the key to acquiring a bigger-than-average fleet in the early-to-middle single-player missions. And, in a multiplayer game, nothing hurts opponents quite like forcing them to watch their prized Heavy Cruisers being led away to your Mothership."

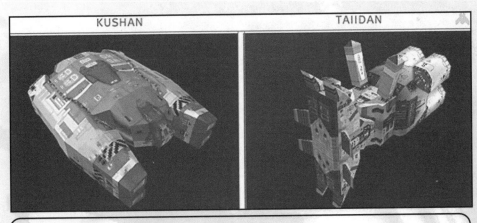

Fig. 1-10. Salvage Corvette

Weaknesses

Slow, so you must be smart about when and how you deploy them. Can't outrun angry pursuers. No firepower.

Using It Best

- Reinl: "Park in dust clouds and jump on unsuspecting harvesters. Also good for sneaking behind and stealing large enemy vessels attacking your Mothership."
- Hamilton: "The Torsten Maneuvers." (See Reinl's comment.)
- Mason: "Hide them in a group of other ships and order the group to attack a target. As soon as your Salvage Corvettes slip in and attach themselves to the target, halt your other ships' attack."

Multigun Corvette

Strengths

Six swiveling guns! Thus, excellent firepower and coverage. Great against Strike craft. Really pops those pesky Scouts.

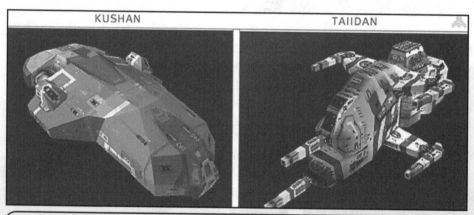

| KUSHAN | TAIIDAN |

Fig. 1-11. Multigun Corvette

Weaknesses

Six *small* guns! Thus, not so great against bigger ships. And it's far down the technology tree, so it takes awhile before you can build them.

Using It Best

- Reinl: "Awesome escort. Use Multigun Corvettes to guard harvesting operations, or any big ship that has trouble against Strike craft."

- Nautikus: "These will wreak absolute havoc on groups of enemy Fighters."
- Mason: "Put them in Claw formation and unleash them against enemy Strike craft. (And retire those lame Heavy Corvettes once you have these.)"
- Hamilton: "Strike craft removal."

Minelayer Corvette

Strengths

Can lay mines right at the enemy's doorstep. Also very effective against harvesting operations. As Chris Mason says, "Leaves little teeny presents for the enemy: they're small, so human opponents may not see them in time."

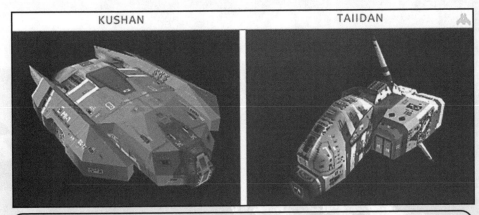

Fig. 1-12. Minelayer Corvette

Weaknesses

No offensive weapons. Fragile. Mason adds, "Space is a big place, and often your little 4-by-4 wall of mines will never be encountered."

Using It Best

- Reinl: "Mine enemy avenues of approach, dust clouds, and other resource concentrations."
- Nautikus: "I agree. Drop 'em in resource pockets."

Frigate Class

Assault Frigate

Strengths

Erinn Hamilton says, "None." But others find it good against Strike craft, especially Corvettes, because it can track targets with its turrets. Turrets also allow the Assault Frigate to fire when it's moving.

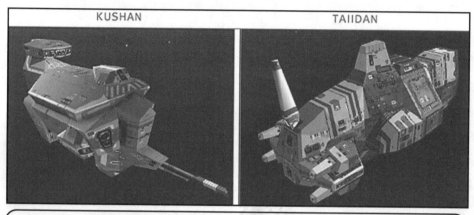

| KUSHAN | TAIIDAN |

Fig. 1-13. Assault Frigate

Weaknesses

Not a whole lot of firepower. Torsten Reinl says, "Good for small fights, but outgunned in large battles."

Using It Best

- Reinl: "Use as early assault and/or heavy escort craft."
- Mason: "Build a few while you're waiting for Ion Cannon Frigates, just in case. Plus, Mission 4, 'Great Wastelands,' is impossible without at least a few of these."
- Hamilton: "Don't use."

Ion Cannon Frigate

Strengths

The backbone of any decent fleet—and a real favorite, as the following comments attest.

Nautikus: "Oooh, yeah! Excellent firepower concentrated into a beam of incandescent fury."

Reinl: "Let's face it. It's sexy."

Mason: "Big Ion Fun! Once you build some of these, you can start thinking about taking down enemy Motherships."

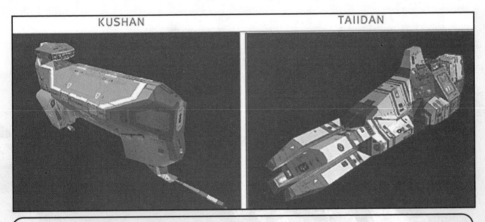

Fig. 1-14. Ion Cannon Frigate

Weaknesses

Low maneuverability. No turret means low coverage. The ion beam tracks slowly because the ship has to move its entire hull to aim and shoot. Thus, it's ineffective against nimble Strike craft. "Can be picked apart by Fighters," Reinl says.

And here's a tip from Falko Poiker, designer of four of *Homeworld*'s single-player missions: "If you're going to micromanage your Capital ships—that is, move your ships as you attack—then Ion Cannon Frigates have real drawbacks. They fire only when they've finished a move, because they have to line up the shot first." The much-maligned Assault Frigates, on the other hand, can fire their turreted guns even when they're broadside to the opponent.

Using It Best

- Reinl: "Best medium, all-purpose assault craft. Can do just about any job."
- Nautikus: "Good against harvesters, Capital ships, and Motherships."
- Mason: "Use in any attacking or defensive role, usually in Wall formation. Not great for harvester escort duty, though, due to its low maneuverability."

Support Frigate

Strengths

Allows repair and refuel of Strike craft far from home. It repairs Capital Ships at 200 points a second.

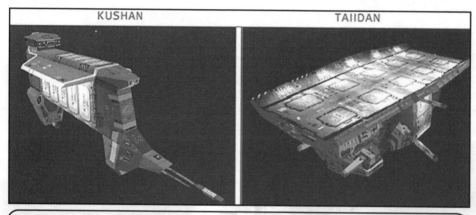

Fig. 1-15. Support Frigate

Weaknesses

Paltry defensive fire.

Using It Best

- Reinl: "Use a Support Frigate to escort a fleet and as a base for Fighters. Or park it in a dust cloud as a forward base for Strike craft."
- Nautikus: "In big maps, place at midway points to refuel Fighters."
- It can also ferry Strike craft through hyperspace.

Drone Frigate (Kushan Only)

Strengths

Provides an awesome anti-Fighter screen for any ship it guards.

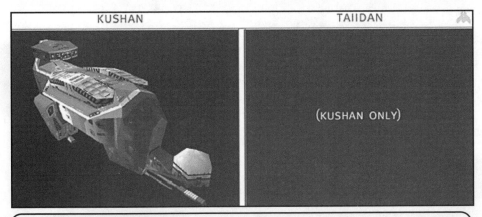

Fig. 1-16. Drone Frigate

Weaknesses

Other than its drones, it has no firepower. Almost useless against enemy Capital ships. Nautikus adds, "With 25 models for every Drone Frigate (one Frigate and 24 drones), building a bunch may tax slow computer systems."

Using It Best

Guard big ships taking heavy fire from swarms of Strike craft.

Defense Field Frigate (Taiidan Only)

Strengths

Same as Drone Frigate. Good anti-Fighter escort. It can deflect all bullets and plasma bombs.

Weaknesses

Same as Drone Frigate. Useful only against Fighters, generally. Useless against ion beams, missles, and mines.

KUSHAN	TAIIDAN

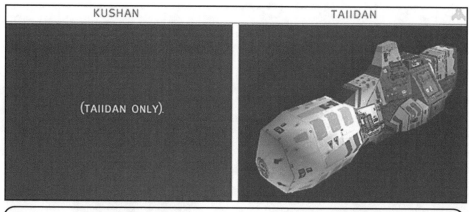

(TAIIDAN ONLY).

Fig. 1-17. Defense Field Frigate

Using It Best

Same as Drone Frigate. Guard bigger ships taking heavy Strike craft fire.

Super Capital Class

Destroyer

Strengths

Massive firepower, with ion cannons *and* rotating turrets for decent coverage, plus good armor. Can dish out some serious damage.

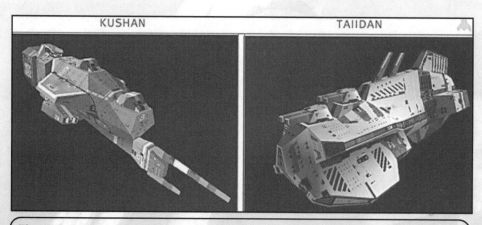

Fig. 1-18. Destroyer

Weaknesses

Slow. Even with turrets, can be ineffective against smaller Strike craft. Relatively expensive to build. Nautikus says, "You can't afford to make as many as you'd probably like to."

Using It Best

- Reinl: "Your premier heavy assault vessel. Use for heavy ship-to-ship battles and for hitting enemy Motherships and Carriers."
- Nautikus: "Use it to destroy anything bigger than a Corvette."

Missile Destroyer

Strengths

Fires homing missiles! Rarely misses its target. Can shred formations of Fighters in no time. Says Nautikus, "If you have one or two of these, you're basically immune to Fighter attack." Or, as Chris Mason puts it, "Missiles = dead Strike craft."

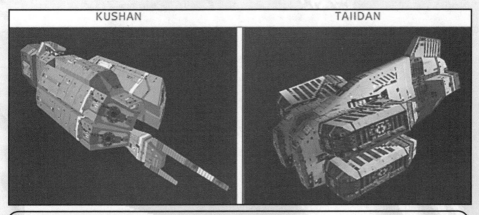

Fig. 1-19. Missile Destroyer

Weaknesses

Less effective against standard Destroyers or groups of Ion Cannon Frigates. Nautikus says, "One-on-one, the standard Destroyer will always win."

Using It Best

- Reinl: "Your premier anti–Strike craft vessel. Take it anywhere you expect heavy Strike craft opposition. *Don't leave home without it.*"
- Nautikus: "That's right. Use it as an escort to keep Fighters off your fleet."
- Mason: "I use these primarily in a defensive role, to mow down incoming Strike craft. Combine two of these with two Grav Well Generators guarding your Mothership and you won't have to worry about enemy Strike Craft. Also very effective at taking out mines. A must for Mission 10, 'Super Nova Research Station.'"

Carrier
Strengths

This "mini-Mothership" can build ships up to Frigate class. Serves as home if your Mothership is destroyed in a multiplayer game.

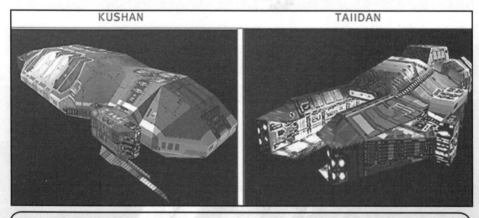

KUSHAN | TAIIDAN

Fig. 1-20. Carrier

Weaknesses

Low firepower for its size means barely adequate self-defense. Can't build Capital ships.

Using It Best

- Reinl: "Use a Carrier to carry large numbers of Strike craft into battle. In multiplayer games, use it as an alternative base if the Mothership dies."

- Mason: "In multiplayer games, I use these to hyperspace Strike craft across the map. Also, I like the look on my opponents' faces when they take out my Mothership—only to discover I have a loaded Carrier hiding at the edge of the map. Oops. *I'm still alive.*"

Heavy Cruiser

Strengths

Wow. The big boy. Can beat anything one-on-one.

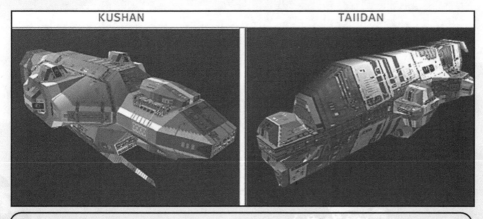

Fig. 1-21. Heavy Cruiser

Weaknesses

Very, very expensive. Very lengthy construction time. And very slow. Says Torsten Reinl, "It's the lumbering giant that can crush a house but couldn't hit a fly."

Using It Best

- Reinl: "Awesome as a Capital ship–killer and a Mothership assault vessel. But use a Heavy Cruiser only in conjunction with escorts! Don't waste RUs building one unless you know what to do with it."
- Nautikus: "Kill! Maim! Destroy!"
- Mason: "Attack things with it."

Noncombat Class

Resource Collector

Strengths

Gets the RUs you need for fleet construction. Decent armor for a Noncombat craft. Can refuel Strike craft.

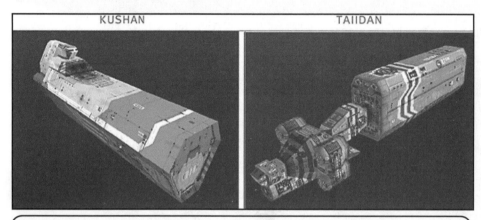

KUSHAN	TAIIDAN

Fig. 1-22. Resource Collector

Weaknesses

No guns. Does not autorepair. And, Chris Mason says, "It attracts enemies looking to slash your income like flies to, uh, honey."

Using It Best

- Reinl: "Send Collectors out *immediately* to collect resources. Don't let them sit around."

- Nautikus: "Alternative to its obvious use—it makes a good kamikaze vessel. It's the largest ship with kamikaze capabilities. Hurts a lot when it hits."

- Mason: "Build 'em, tell 'em to harvest, and guard 'em. And get some Resource Controllers into play fast."

Resource Controller

Strengths

Greatly improves harvesting efficiency. Its docking pads allow it to refuel six Fighters and two Corvettes at once.

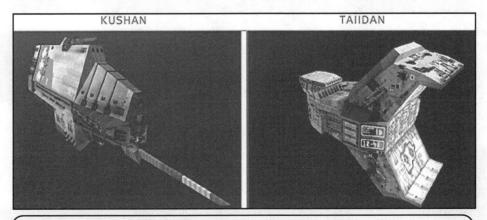

KUSHAN	TAIIDAN

Fig. 1-23. Resource Controller

Weaknesses

Can't defend itself. Needs protection.

Using It Best

- Reinl: "Order each Controller to guard one or two Collectors to significantly reduce RU delivery times."
- Mason: "Personally, I like to use a 2 Collector–to–1 Controller ratio. If you tell the Controller to guard both Collectors, it will stay equidistant between the two."

Probe

Strengths

Cheap spy tool. Incredibly fast.

Weaknesses

"None, unless you expect it to do anything other than what it's designed for," says Torsten Reinl. You can use its engine only once, though, so select its destination carefully.

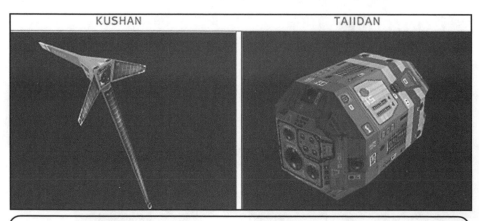

Fig. 1-24. Probe

Using It Best

- Reinl: "Check up on your enemies at any point in a game."
- Nautikus: "General annoyance. People hate being probed."
- Mason: "Fire off a Probe at any hyperspace destination before you jump to make sure no nasty surprises await you."

Cloak Generator
Strengths
Can cloak small fleets when grouped with them.

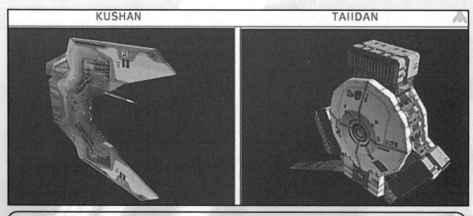

Fig. 1-25. Cloak Generator

Weaknesses
Far down in technology tree.

Using It Best

- Mason: "Cloak Generators recover their charge at about one-half the rate they use it. So if you combine three Cloak Generators (trust me on the math) and stagger their use, you can keep ships cloaked indefinitely. An absolute *must* to get by Mission 14, 'Bridge of Sighs.'"

- Reinl: "I rarely use it. I prefer my enemies to see what's about to kill them."

Grav Well Generator

Strengths

Immobilizes Strike craft, making them easy targets. Also inhibits enemy hyperspace jumps into the area. You don't know what hell is until you've flown a big, potent wing of Strike craft into a gravity well.

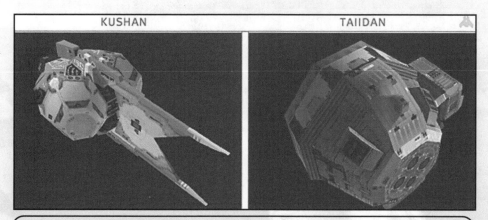

| KUSHAN | TAIIDAN |

Fig. 1-26. Grav Well Generator

Weaknesses

No guns. Immobile Strike craft with turrets can still target it. Once it burns out, it blows up.

Using It Best

- Reinl: "Take a Grav Well Generator and a Cloak Generator with a small fleet and go hunting for Strike craft."

- Nautikus: "Use anytime you want to prevent hyperspace jumps."

- Mason: "Use with a Missile Destroyer to devastate Strike craft wings. Also, in multiplayer games, it provides your only defense against enemy ships hyperspacing into your area. Keep a few around and look for that purple ping in the Sensors Manager."

Proximity Sensor

Strengths

Starts beeping when cloaked bad boys are near. Speedy and highly maneuverable.

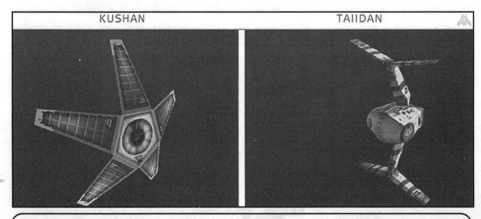

KUSHAN   TAIIDAN

Fig. 1-27. Proximity Sensor

Weaknesses

Little armor. Easy to destroy.

Using It Best

Keep them around the Mothership or deploy with fleets to reveal enemy sneak attacks. "Order a Proximity Sensor to guard your main defensive fleet," says Mason. "That way, your forces fighting off the cloaked intruders will always be near or in a Proximity field."

Sensors Array

Strengths

Lets you see every ship on the map. Gives you a far more accurate picture of what's "out there."

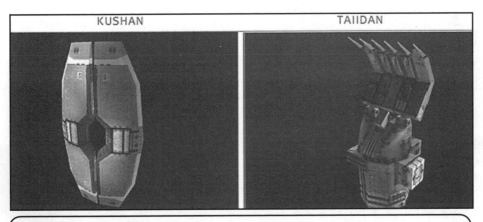

Fig. 1-28. Sensors Array

Weaknesses

Far down the technology tree.

Using It Best

Mason: "Build it. Protect it. As long as you have it, you operate at a much higher level of intel."

Research Ship

Strengths

You're dead without it. Plus, as Chris Mason says, "It thinks up new stuff for you to play with."

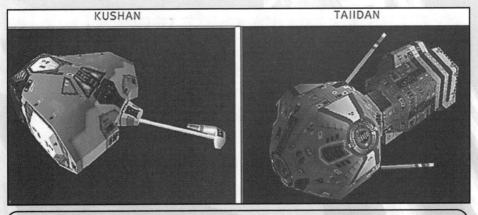

Fig. 1-29. Research Ship

Weaknesses

No guns. Requires protection.

Using It Best

- Never let a Research Ship sit idle!
- Build at least three, so the linked station has enough aggregate armor to withstand enemy raiding parties.
- Mason: "Build as many as you can, as fast as you can. Keep them working continuously whenever possible."

ATTACKING

In this section, we asked our experts to outline a few of their favorite offensive tactics—how they deploy ships, what attack formations they prefer, how they designate targets, and so on.

Strike Craft Tactics

Strike craft—Fighters and Corvettes—are small, quick-hitting ships that are deadliest grouped in large swarms. Here's some advice on how to use yours most effectively, and how best to knock out the enemy's.

The key to effective Strike-craft tactics is SUPERIOR NUMBERS.

This may seem obvious, but as a game progresses and fleets begin to swell in size and firepower, Strike craft flying alone or in small groups might as well be charcoal briquettes. Sure, you can send an occasional speedy Scout (set to Evasive tactics) to spy on enemy maneuvers, but, in general, Strike craft should travel in sizeable swarms arrayed in Claw or X formation. (We'll cover Sphere formation later.)

Fig. 1-30. Fighters rely on speed and numbers to attack effectively.

"My basic Strike Group consists of 20 Scouts and 20 Interceptors for ambush," says Erinn Hamilton. "Then I add six to 12 Heavy Corvettes and (when available) six to 12 Multigun Corvettes for escort." This configuration lets you pounce quickly on primary targets with a large swarm of highly maneuverable Fighters. Your escorting Corvettes, in turn, chew up the primary target's escorts, leaving your Fighters free to attack with impunity. When huge numbers aren't an option, micro-management is the key to effective Strike craft use.

Early on, deploy Strike Groups against your enemy's resource collection and/or research operations.

The early phase of any game usually features a race between opponents to harvest a cache of RUs and to research better technology. Form a Strike Group geared to hit these enemy operations. If your raiders find an undefended or lightly guarded Resource Collector or Research Ship, concentrate fire on the primary target in Sphere formation for maximum effect.

Later in a game, of course, you're more likely to run into a cloud of escorts, too. In this case, you need a contingent of Corvettes to guard your attack sphere of Fighters; otherwise, you're better off dragging a "group attack" box around the entire enemy squadron (primary target *and* its escorts) and attacking in Claw formation.

"Strike Craft are most effective at attacking resource operations, I think," says Chris Mason. "Resource Collectors take such irregular paths while harvesting, so you need ships with maneuverability and speed to hunt them down."

Mason's favorite mix for this task is 10 to 20 Attack Bombers in a Sphere formation to pound on the Resource Collector or Controller, escorted by several Multigun Corvettes in a Delta, X, or Claw formation, to take out hostile Strike craft escorting the enemy harvesters.

"Of course," he adds, "Attack Bombers and Multigun Corvettes are pretty far down their respective technology trees." His "poor man's" version— Interceptors and Heavy Corvettes.

Use Sphere formation to attack slow or poorly defended targets.

Again, the drawback to using a Fighter or Corvette is its lack of firepower. Against enemy Strike craft, this is no problem; they're lightly armored. But against Capital ships' thicker hulls you need a big Strike Group, with all guns trained on the target.

If your Strike Group encounters, say, a lightly guarded Resource Controller or a wandering Ion Cannon Frigate, attack in Sphere formation. This pours an uninterrupted stream of fire into the center of the sphere, taking out the target quickly. Sphere formation can be effective against even the most powerful Capital ships—as long as they have no appreciable escort.

Chris Mason agrees. "Sphere is a great formation for Strike Groups to concentrate fire on bigger ships," he says. "It can work against Strike craft, too, but be careful. If the enemy gets a sphere around yours, you'd better change plans fast."

Use Claw formation against enemy Strike craft or well-guarded Capital ships.

Again, your Strike Group is speedy but lightly armored. If you encounter equally maneuverable enemy craft, or a situation with lots of hostile fire (as in a big fleet-to-fleet battle), the relatively stationary Sphere formation can spell disaster. Instead, keep your Strike Group on the move in the deadly Claw formation.

Fig. 1-31. Claw is the best pure attack formation for large groups of Fighters, such as these Interceptors.

Says Chris Mason, "Maybe it's the name or the way it looks, but I usually keep my Strike craft in Claw formation when attacking other Strike craft or whenever I want to retain the mobility I lose with Sphere formation."

Counter enemy Fighter swarms with Multigun Corvettes or, later in the game, Missile Destroyers.

Thick enemy Fighter swarms can be a real annoyance in any phase of a game. The Multigun Corvette is the best anti–Fighter craft in your fleet. The technology you need (Fast-tracking Turrets) is a few steps down the research tree. But as soon as you can build this six-gun Fighter-killer, crank out a handful for escort duty.

Fig. 1-32. Few things are as beautiful (or effective) as a volley of missiles launched into the teeth of an enemy Fighter formation.

Most Capital ship weapons systems are too slow to thin out swirling Fighter wings. But the Missile Destroyer is a fearsome exception. Its volleys of guided missiles can tear through a Fighter squadron in short order. Keep a couple of Missile Destroyers in your Battle Groups for insurance.

Always "group attack" enemy Fighters with your Heavy or Multigun Corvettes.

Most often you'll want to use concentrated fire on enemy targets—that is, hit targets one at a time with every gun in your selected group. But, as Chris Mason points out, "The exception to this is when I'm using Heavy or Multigun Corvettes. Because the strength of these units is their multiple targeting, it would be a waste to focus on just one target."

Instead, direct your Multigun Corvettes to "group attack" enemy Fighters by dragging a box around the enemy swarm. "It's fun to pick a pack of targets and watch the carnage—or better yet, fire-and-forget and move on to other tasks," says Mason.

In a game's later phases, consider using Scouts for kamikaze attacks.

Scouts have incredibly wimpy guns and armor. But a Scout flying headlong into an enemy ship can hurt so good. When asked how he likes to attack with his Strike craft, tester Nautikus replied, "One word—kamikaze. OK, it's a cheap shot, and it gets you called all kinds of names. But it's a lot of fun."

Capital Ship Tactics

Things change when you add Capital ships to your arsenal, and for good reason. Few things are as glorious as the sight of a Heavy Cruiser, guns blazing, lighting up near space like a mininova. But you'd better know how to group and deploy your big boys, or you may lose them to a swarm of little boys in a most humiliating fashion.

Draw enemy fire with decoys.

Ion Cannon Frigates, Destroyers, and Heavy Cruisers pack a serious punch. So when your Capital ships engage enemy Capital ships, you want to get in the first licks. A good tactic: if your Probes or Scouts locate a group of big, hostile gunships, send a few wings of Strike craft set to Evasive tactics ahead of your own Capital ships.

Says Torsten Reinl, "While enemy Frigates and Super Capital ships swing around to aim their ungainly guns at your nimble Fighters, slip in your own big-hitters from behind or the side. Then squeeze off a few unchallenged volleys before your targets can react."

Use the "Wall" as your Capital ship attack formation.

This tip is absolutely fundamental, for two related reasons. First, Wall formation keeps your ships from hitting each other in a fleet-to-fleet melee. Second, it gives you the best alignment for concentrated attack, giving every gun in the group a clear line of fire to the single target.

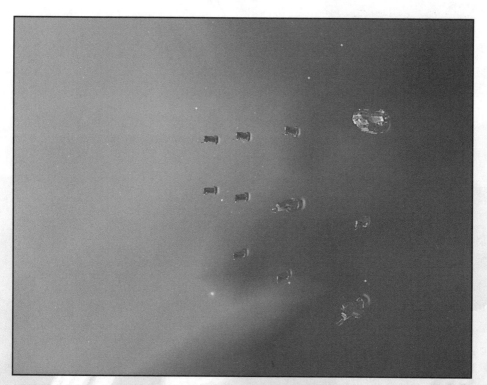

Fig. 1-33. A powerful armada in Wall formation is a majestic sight—but it's not just for show.

"Wall formation definitely gives you the best bang for the buck," says Torsten Reinl.

In Capital ship combat, concentrated fire is your best targeting option.

In fact, the Sierra testers see this as the *only* way to go. "In an otherwise equal battle, you can win by directing your entire group to take out enemy ships one by one," says Nautikus. If you simply drag a 'group attack' box around a hostile fleet, you usually lose, unless your force is considerably stronger."

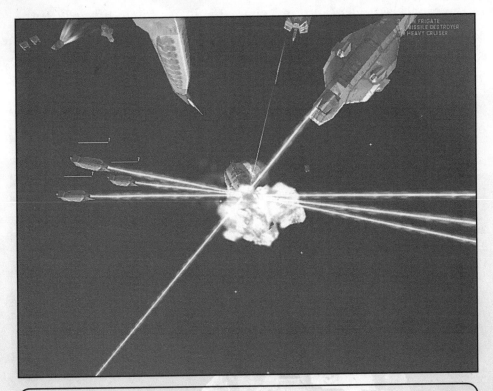

Fig. 1-34. Order all Capital ships in a group to attack the same target for a quick knockout.

Why? Concentrated fire kills ships quickly. Suppose your opponent executes a "group attack" against your fleet while you concentrate your fire on enemy ships, one by one. More of your ships take damage than the enemy's, but yours survive far longer. When your concentrated fire knocks out an enemy ship, you eliminate the incoming fire that now-dead ship was directing at one of your vessels. As you destroy target after target, you reduce your opponent's aggregate firepower while yours stays the same, despite ship damage.

Thus, at the end of such a battle, you may have a lot of *damaged* Capital ships. But they repair themselves eventually. On the other hand, your opponent's *destroyed* Capital ships are gone forever. As Chris Mason puts it, "With the idea that the sooner a single enemy ship goes down, the sooner one less ship is firing at my ships, I *always* use concentrated fire against hostile Capital ships."

Beware (and use) the basic capture maneuver.

One of the most dastardly (and fun) special abilities in *Homeworld* is the Salvage Corvette's ability to "salvage"— that is, steal—Capital ships from the opposing fleet. When salvaged, an enemy ship joins your own fleet. Can you imagine a more delightful scenario?

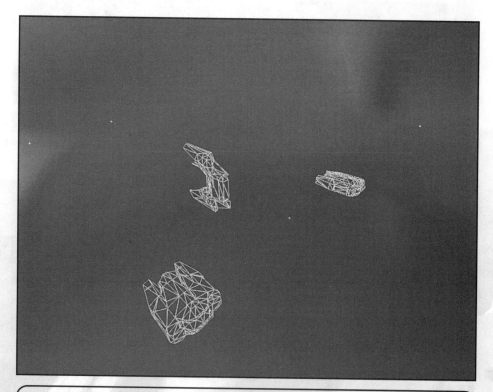

Fig. 1-35. Use cloaked Salvage Corvettes to steal enemy ships and bring them over to your side.

When Erinn Hamilton assembles a Capture Group, he includes two or more Salvage Corvettes and at least three Cloak Generators; then he adds six to 12 Light Corvettes for basic escort. He assigns one number to the whole group, and then assigns separate group numbers to his Salvage Corvettes, Cloak Generators, and Light Corvettes.

"I place the entire group in a Wall Formation," he says, "so a single Cloak Generator can cover the entire group."

Always include a Missile Destroyer or two in your main Battle Group.

We've already discussed how effective Missile Destroyers can be against enemy Strike craft. They also pack a pretty decent wallop against larger targets. This one–two combination is particularly important when your main Battle Group finally attacks an enemy's Mothership.

"When you show up at your enemies' doorsteps, they'll throw *everything they have* at you," says Torsten Reinl. So expect swirling swarms of angry Fighters, as well as a stout defense screen of Capital ships. Missile Destroyers give you flexibility in meeting this double-edged challenge.

"Rumor has it Scouts are inexpensive kamikaze weapons," adds Reinl. "But few Scouts can slip unscathed through a guided missile volley."

Attack enemy Motherships with enough firepower to do the job quickly.

When finally you decide to hit your enemy's big house, you'd better be ready for hell in space. First, you need *lots* of powerful guns to drain 160,000 armor points from a massive Mothership. Second, you need a formidable escort to keep her teeming defense forces at bay. Assemble a Battle Group with as many Ion Cannon Frigates, Destroyers, and Heavy Cruisers as possible. Add two or three Missile Destroyers and plenty of Fighters and Corvettes assigned to guard duty.

"In most cases, I send in my main Battle Group (via hyperspace, if possible), and concentrate all big-gun fire on the Mothership, ignoring any other threats," says Chris Mason. "Even with a good escort, I'll lose a fair number of ships. But if my fleet is big enough, I can destroy the Mothership before her defense force can eliminate all my Capital ships. And thus I win"—as long as the enemy doesn't have a hidden Carrier-based force lurking on the edge of the map.

Against craftier opponents, Mason finds this strategy a little too simple. For instance, if you ignore Salvage Corvettes in a wild multiship melee, they become a big threat to your fleet, simply stealing your Capital ships, one by one. It takes a good escort of Strike craft and a sharp eye to keep Capital ships under your control.

"You may want to bring a Gravity Well Generator or two with you, as well," adds Mason. "Activate one to keep your opponent from hyperspacing the enemy Mothership away just when you think you have it."

DEFENDING

Defense isn't quite as glamorous as offense, but it's just as important. We asked the *Homeworld* testing team to sketch their favorite defensive tactics—how to array forces, which formations work best, how to designate targets, and so on. Our experts focused on two primary areas of defense strategy—escorting big ships (including harvesters) and, of course, defending your Mothership.

Escort Tactics

In earlier sections you learned that even very powerful ships can be vulnerable without proper escort. Some of the following tips on deploying your escort forces reiterate and expand on those tips.

Yes, go ahead and use the special defense-oriented ships for escort duty.

Let's start with the obvious. *Homeworld* fleets feature a number of craft designed specially for defense duty. By all means, include them in your escort groups—especially the ferocious Defenders. Their gimballed guns give them 90 percent coverage, making them deadly trackers of enemy Fighters. Consider the Kushan Drone Frigate, as well; it releases a cloud of 24 tenacious little drones that will peck to death enemy Strike craft in the area.

Less deadly, but still effective, are the Taiidan-only Defense Fighter and Defense Field Frigate. These feature no attack weaponry whatsoever; alone, they can't thin out ranks of enemy attackers. Yet they can deflect most incoming enemy fire (except for ion beams and missiles). Used together with, say, a contingent of Multigun Corvettes (see the following tip), these special defense units can provide a nearly impenetrable escort screen against enemy Strike craft.

Nothing kicks Fighter butt like an escort of Multigun Corvettes.

It bears repeating: Multigun Corvettes, with six swiveling guns each sporting the fabulous Fast-tracking Turret technology, are the bane of attacking Fighter squadrons.

In general, Strike Craft make awesome escorts.

So says tester Chris Mason. He likes Strike craft escorts for several reasons. "First, you can build them simultaneously with the bigger ships they'll guard," he says. "Second, they're quick enough to get back to their charge if the battle takes them away from it. Third, if all else fails, you can kamikaze Strike craft into attacking ships as a last-ditch effort to save the more valuable ships they're guarding."

Use the Sphere formation as a defensive cocoon.

"The Sphere formation is, of course, my choice for guarding anything," says Sierra tester Nautikus. Keep in mind, however, that Sphere isn't always the most effective *combat* formation. A Fighter escort (even set to Evasive tactics) suffers more damage in Sphere than in the more mobile Claw or X.

On the other hand, in Claw or X, the entire escort group swings back and forth in formation, making passes at attackers and leaving their assigned ship with each pass. They also form up on only one side of the ship they're guarding, leaving the other sides unshielded and open to attack.

Fig. 1-36. Multigun Corvettes guarding in Sphere formation are a nearly impenetrable shield against enemy Fighter attacks.

Sphere formation, on the other hand, places defenders completely around the guarded ship; they stay there even in the heat of combat, so your escorts won't dodge as much fire, but they also shield the ship they're guarding. And that's the whole idea of an escort, isn't it?

NOTE

Keep in mind that Corvettes are good at detroying Fighters, Capital Ships pulverise Corvettes, and Fighters can blast Capital Ships. This "circle of death" can help you choose what targets are appropratie for your ships.

Include a few Repair Corvettes in any major escort group.

For obvious reasons, few escort screens are perfectly bulletproof. The valuable ships you guard inevitably will take *some* damage. Accelerate their healing with a Repair Corvette or two. (We suggest you assign more than one to your escort force. Repair Corvettes aren't sturdy, and expire promptly when caught in a vicious firefight.)

Add a cloaked Grav Well Generator to escort groups to surprise enemy Strike craft.

Escort groups can make good use of Cloak and Grav Well Generators, especially when you use them in combination. Group the two generators in formation and order them to guard likely targets of enemy Strike craft—Resource Controllers, Ion Cannon Frigate groups—or just attach them to your main Battle Group.

When your sensors detect enemy Fighters making an attack run, quickly fire up the Cloak Generator to hide the Grav Well Generator; then activate the gravity well. Attacking Strike craft looking to swarm with impunity suddenly find themselves stuck in gravity's mudhole, and become sitting ducks for your escort gunships.

Defending the Mothership

The most important thing you'll defend in any game of *Homeworld* is your Mothership. The easy way is to press [E] to select all friendly ships in the viewing area, and then order the whole motley family to guard Mom. Of course, this is anything but the most *effective* way. When big bad guys float into the neighborhood, heed the following advice.

Fig. 1-37. If you spot an enemy Battle Group making a major push, lay mines across its primary approach route to your Mothership.

Lay mines across obvious approach routes.

This is always fun. Torsten Reinl says, "If I have a pretty good idea where the enemy's coming from, laying mines is the first step." He claims he's had opponents break off attacks because half their assault force was lost or seriously damaged in his minefield.

Balance your Defense Group well.

You never know what a wily opponent may send at you, so your defense forces had better be effective against as many types of threat as possible. Erinn Hamilton's favorite Mothership Defense Group includes at least eight Ion Cannon Frigates in Wall formation to fend off Capital-class ships; a full complement of 20 Defenders to keep incoming Strike craft at bay; two to six Grav Well Generators to immobilize swarms of Strike craft, and six to 12 Proximity Sensors (set in Sphere formation around the Mothership) to unveil sneaky cloaked attacks.

Chris Mason adds a few Missile Destroyers to help decimate Strike craft swarms; their missiles are particularly deadly against Fighters frozen in a gravity well. Torsten Reinl suggests keeping a few Salvage Corvettes handy, too. "Chris's biggest nightmare is getting his fleets stolen when he comes to attack me," he insists.

Last, but not least, don't forget the big boy…

Park a Heavy Cruiser next door.

Late in a game, it's so very, very nice to have at least one Heavy Cruiser counterpunching enemy Battle Groups making their big rush. Sure, Cruisers are slow and expensive. But speed isn't an issue when you're defending your stationary Mothership. And by the endgame phase, you should have RUs to burn.

"Heavy Cruisers are beautiful," says Torsten Reinl. "Not only can they dish it out, they can take a *lot* of punishment before they die." Reinl also points out that Heavy Cruisers make very good distractions, drawing enemy fire and buying you time to send in reinforcements—or jump your Mothership out of harm's way.

Turn your Super Capital ships to face the threat WELL BEFORE its final approach.

Destroyers and Heavy Cruisers have killer gun racks, but their turning speed is excruciatingly slow. Thus, a simple but critical concern when positioning your defense forces is that your Super Capital-class ships face the correct way. As tester Chris Mason says, "There's nothing worse than seeing a slew of enemy Ion Cannon Frigates pounding on your Destroyers as they *slo-o-o-owly* turn to face the threat."

To avoid such a fiasco, keep a sharp eye out for approaching red blips on your sensors. When something wicked this way comes, immediately deploy a Probe or Scout to take a peek. If it's a serious threat, your big ships should have plenty of time to face up.

Concentrate your fire on the biggest threats first.

Yes, it takes a lot of heat to knock out a Super Capital ship. But remember, one Heavy Cruiser packs the firepower of almost *five* Ion Cannon Frigates. To quote the gameplay guide, "This bruiser carries four twin-mounted ion cannons and six heavy turrets, each almost half the size of an entire Frigate." Destroyers feature four massive guns, as well.

When defending your Mothership, give top priority to removing such megathreats as soon as possible. Concentrate the fire of your entire defense fleet on enemy Super Capital ships first, starting with the biggest, and take them out one at a time. It may seem like you're thinning enemy Battle Group ranks awfully slowly. But remember, it's the number of *guns* you eliminate that counts, not the number of *ships*.

To be fair, this approach is open to debate among *Homeworld* testers. Chris Mason prefers to throw everything he has at the enemy's *smallest* Capital ships first. He explains, "I want to start reducing the size of his fleet ASAP, and it can take too long to take out a Heavy Cruiser."

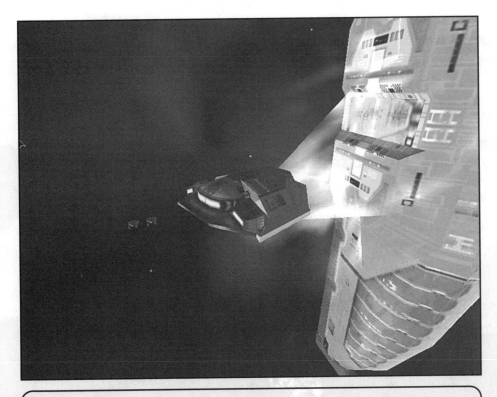

Fig. 1-38. Keep a contingent of Repair Corvettes near your Mothership. They can slow her deterioration when enemy Battle Groups hit hard.

Stanch the bleeding with Repair Corvettes.

As recommended in earlier "The *Homeworld* Fleet" section, the moment your Mothership comes under heavy fire, you should order a handful of Repair Corvettes to repair her. They probably can't offset fully the massive damage the enemy's thundering Battle Group inflicts. But they may slow hull degradation enough to let your Defense Group eliminate the threat before the Mothership dies.

HARVESTING

It goes without saying that you can't build a mighty *Homeworld* fleet without RU's. (Gee, looks like we said it anyway.) Harvesting plentiful resources—and disrupting the enemy's harvest—often can trump even the most cleverly devised combat strategies and maneuvers.

Again, we turn to our veteran advisors: *How do you deploy and defend your resourcing operations? How much emphasis do you put on disrupting your enemy's resource collection?*

Deploying Your Collectors

Just tell 'em to go harvest, right? Wrong. Deploying your resource craft intelligently is critical to a successful campaign.

Never let Resource Collectors sit idle.

Idle Resource Collectors might as well be space junk. Check the area near your Mothership from time to time. Be sure all new or recently deployed Collectors are actively harvesting.

Always order Resource Controllers to "guard" Resource Collectors.

This is one of those fundamental *Homeworld* tactics that everyone should employ, regardless of the game type. Resource Controllers are valuable time-savers, but only if you deploy them close to Collectors. The best way to ensure this proximity is to order Controllers to guard Collectors.

"I always assign one Controller to guard each Collector," says Nautikus. "That way, as soon as the harvester is full, it can drop off its load immediately."

Fellow tester Chris Mason employs a similar trick. "Generally, I order one Controller to guard two Collectors, which keeps the Controller equidistant between the two Collectors."

Attacking Enemy Collectors

The *Homeworld* testers offered distinctly different opinions about attacking enemy resource operations. Choose the approach that best suits your own style of play.

Start hitting harvesters right away, and keep hitting them the entire game.

Some players pump out Scouts and start taking down enemy harvesters from the very beginning; then they never stop. This is the Arkansas-basketball game-play philosophy—full-court pressure from buzzer to buzzer. Or, as tester Nautikus puts it, "A penny destroyed is a penny earned." It requires a lot of careful micromanagement and regular use of Probe reconnaissance, but it can be most satisfying and very effective.

"Every harvester you can kill, capture, or confuse is that much less money the enemy has," says Nautikus. "If the enemy is foolish enough to deploy an unprotected harvesting operation, you can have a *lot* of fun. Also, if you're playing in a game with Bounties active, unprotected harvesters are easy money."

Or you can bide your time.

Lead tester Torsten Reinl prefers this strategy. Instead of sending Scouts to chase Resource Collectors around the map—the equivalent of launching aggressive pawn-versus-pawn attacks early in a chess game—he suggests you sit back and focus on developing your fleet. Later, when you have more powerful raiders at your disposal—Interceptors grouped with combat Corvettes and even Frigates—you can launch swift and devastating attacks on enemy harvesting operations.

"I tend to go after enemy collectors only after the game has progressed a bit," says Reinl. "I can only harass and disrupt enemy RU collection at the beginning, but I can virtually shut it down later in the game. Early on, I don't care if my opponent can build a bunch of Strike craft or research labs. It's the bigger ships later that can ruin your day."

In multiplayer games, where maps are small and resources less plentiful (and thus more precious), however, Reinl suggests you harass at least one enemy's Collectors right from the start.

Or you can simply ignore enemy Collectors (unless they encroach on your "territory").

This is the *bring-it-on* philosophy of gameplay. Forget the preliminary sniping and skirmishing. You build your fleet, I build mine; then let's line 'em up and may the best player win. Tester Chris Mason, for example, wages successful campaigns without worrying much about enemy resource operations.

"No, I don't go out of my way to get at the enemy's RU collection," he says. As long as his own operations are well-protected, Mason is perfectly willing to concede a share of resources to his opponents. But Mason is aggressive in a territorial sense. "I do attack anything that comes into the nearby resource clusters I designate as mine," he admits.

Steal enemy Collectors to boost your harvest.

Why destroy things you can use? Killing collectors may cripple the enemy's fleet development, but *swiping* them does the same thing, accelerating your own fleet development in the process. And it's so deliciously *humiliating*.

Torsten Reinl is a big proponent of this tactic. "My first move, always, is to steal a Collector or two using Salvage Corvettes," he says. Naturally, this works best early on, before enough escort craft exist to protect enemy harvesters properly.

Hit enemy Controllers first, but don't ignore the Collectors.

If your Strike Group finds a busy enemy "collection center"—multiple Resource Collectors dumping loads of RUs into a Resource Controller—focus your initial attack on the Controller. Eliminating Controllers slows the collection process significantly.

Once the Controller is dust, be sure to destroy some Collectors, too. They'll scatter, so you might not catch them all. But each one you eliminate means one less load of RUs—the equivalent of eliminating a Frigate or half a Destroyer. Plus, it won't take long for your opponent to crank out a new Controller and get it in position.

When you do hit, hit HARD and FAST.

Resource Collectors and Controllers are relatively well-armored; they can take enough punishment to survive until help arrives. In fact, bloody resource battles often start as minor skirmishes that quickly escalate as both sides throw in reinforcements. To avoid such a scenario, build an attack force lethal enough to do the job fast.

"When I hit harvesters, I want my forces strong enough to persuade the enemy to abandon them and retreat," says Torsten Reinl. "The second the enemy sees my ships, I want the outcome already determined: I win."

Quick search-and-destroy raids with a wing of 20 Interceptors are effective in the early going. In fact, tester Erinn Hamilton uses his Strike Groups almost exclusively for antiharvesting. Later in a game, add some bigger guns to your raiding party and seek enemy collection centers.

"Should I be lucky enough to find an entire group of Collectors and Controllers," says Reinl, "I throw in a swarm of Attack Bombers or a few Ion Cannon Frigates, and maybe even a Destroyer or two."

Fig. 1-39. Attack Bombers attacking in Sphere formation are particularly lethal against Resource Collectors or Controllers.

Throw Attack Bombers at harvesters.

Says Torsten Reinl, "Twenty Attack Bombers in Sphere or Wall formation are a harvester's worst nightmare."

Indeed, Attack Bombers are particularly well-suited to raiding enemy resourcers. They're fast enough to roam in packs and hunt slow harvesters. Yet their plasma bomb launchers let them penetrate thick Resource Controller and Collector armor much faster than their light-gunned brethren in the Fighter class.

"It's still relatively slow and fragile," warns Reinl. "But it packs quite a punch."

Defending Your Collectors

While your raiders traipse about slaughtering enemy harvesters, don't neglect your own resource activities. Here are a few tips on how best to protect your valuable rock-suckers.

Guard your harvesters.

Duh.

But I had to say it. Keep a modest contingent of Fighters on guard duty, preferably in Sphere formation, around each resource ship. Add a few Light and/or Heavy Corvettes as they become available, too, to help thin out enemy Fighter swarms.

Add extra escort to Resource Controllers.

Again, a no-brainer. If you assign a Resource Controller to "guard" one or two Collectors (to keep it near them), add a somewhat larger group of Fighters and combat Corvettes in a Sphere formation around the Controller.

"This way the Fighters and Corvettes do double duty," says tester Chris Mason. "They guard the most valuable unit in the group, but they can hustle quickly to any nearby Collector under attack, as well."

Keep a sizeable group of Fighters on standby for emergency rescue.

As games progress, you stretch your forces too thin if you try to assign strong escort units to every harvester that roams a map's far-flung dust clouds and asteroid veins. A better tactic is to deploy a substantial group of fast Fighters near your richest resource area.

"In most maps, I try to keep a large handful of Scouts and/or Interceptors on standby in case I need them to defend a Resource Collector," says Torsten Reinl.

"If my Collectors are mining a faraway resource cluster, I add a second rescue group of Light Corvettes." Light Corvettes are cheap, yet they're good to send in Sphere formation to rescue a harvester. They surround their charge quickly, picking off Fighters and setting up a nice defensive screen.

Park big-gun defenders near collection centers.

Here's the converse of an earlier tip: when opponents stumble on one of your "collection centers"—a rich resource cluster where you have a Controller and multiple Collectors at work—they'll likely hit your operation with big guns as well as Strike craft. Thus, it's a good idea to deploy some Ion Cannon Frigates, and maybe a Destroyer or two, near your Controller.

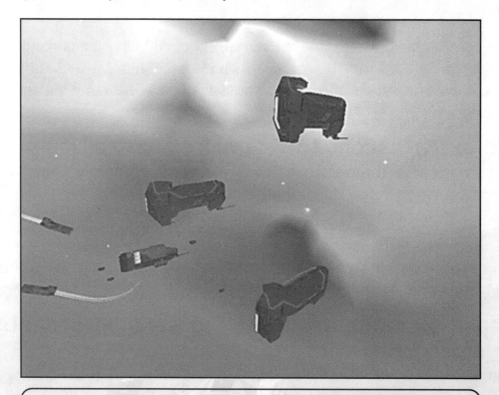

Fig. 1-40. Enemies may target your "collection centers" (a Resource Controller gathering RU loads from multiple harvesters) with big guns. Protect such centers with Capital ships, if necessary.

When in doubt, HYPERSPACE!

Remember, when the Hyperspace option is active in a multiplayer game, you can simply hop your Resource Collectors and Controllers out of danger—if you have enough RUs in the bank.

Nautikus adds, "To speed up resource collection on large maps, I like to hyperspace Collector/Controller duo to distant resource pockets."

CHAPTER 2
MULTIPLAYER
STRATEGIES

Sure, *Homeworld*'s Single Player game is challenging. But let's be honest—it's a training campaign. You spend a few nights hammering your way back to Hiigara. You recover your birthright. You have fun. You win! But then what happens? You spend the next hundred nights getting crushed by friends and strangers in *Homeworld* multiplayer melees.

Why? Because humans are cunning in ways that computer AI may never be. Humans are unpredictable. They deliberately mislead you. They bait and trap. They take unacceptable risks that, shockingly, pay off. They do crazy, sneaky, creative things.

Eventually, yes, you will develop your own effective strategies. But first, you need to master the multiplayer basics and a bit more. That's where this chapter comes in. My consultants, the Sierra Quality Assurance (QA) team assigned to test *Homeworld,* are most likely far better than you are right now. Heed their wisdom and learn. My special thanks goes to Torsten Reinl, QA lead for *Homeworld,* and his awesome QA cohorts—Phil Kuhlmey, Christopher Mason, and Erinn Hamilton—for their cogent and generous input.

THE BIG QUESTION

First things first. Attack tips, defense tactics, special tricks—none of this matters if you don't know how to develop a fleet. So I posed the following question to my panel of experts: "In a standard multiplayer game, how do you assemble effective fleet forces?" Their answers differed in detail but were remarkably similar in terms of overall strategy.

THE ULTIMATE GOAL: BALANCE!

Sierra QA tester Christopher Mason notes, "In a multiplayer match, your goal is to build a fleet that can take out enemy Motherships. To this end, you need ships with Ion Cannons and their bigger, badder cousins, Heavy Guns"—that is, Ion Cannon Frigates, Destroyers, and the biggest of the big boys, the Heavy

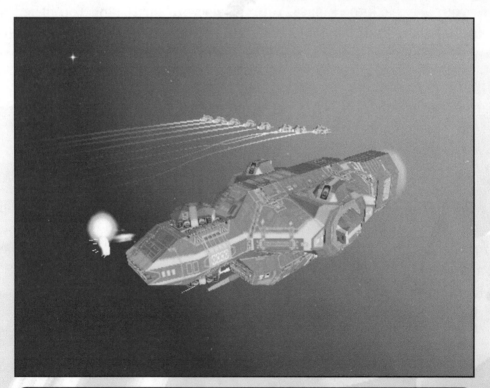

Fig. 2-1. Balance your fleet! If left undefended, Capital Ships—even this hulking Heavy Cruiser—can fall prey to a persistent swarm of tiny Strike Craft.

Cruiser. But Mason also notes that Capital Ships have vulnerabilities. "You can't just focus on heavy firepower if you want to be successful," he says.

Balance is the overall key to success. Yes, you want long hitters in the endgame. But Destroyers and Heavy Cruisers are way, way down the tech tree—that is, you need to spend a lot of time researching many technologies before you can even build these boats. Plus, they're expensive; 3700 RUs for a single Heavy Cruiser is a stiff price to pay for firepower. Thus, you can't get big ships without an extensive and well-defended harvesting operation plus high-powered research facilities.

Plus, as Mason noted above, the big boats have another major drawback: They are almost defenseless against nimble Strike Craft. Nothing is more pathetic and demoralizing than to see one of your expensive Heavy Cruisers slowly pecked to death by a swarm of weensy Attack Bombers. You'd better have enough of your own Strike Craft ready to assign to escort duty.

HOW TO DEVELOP YOUR FLEET

This section sketches some overall guidelines for fleet development in the early, middle, and endgame phases of a standard multiplayer match. Note the word "standard" in the previous sentence. We'll discuss fleet development for some of the special-option multiplayer matches in a later section.

Early Phase: Harvest and Research

As in any real-time strategy (RTS) game, you must start small. But it helps if you start smart, too. Focus on building a good balance of Resource Collectors and Research Ships with enough Scouts to defend both in the early phase of your multiplayer game.

Start harvesting right away.

As the game opens, send any existing Resource Collectors to begin harvesting, and then *immediately* build another Collector and get it working, too. Resources are key to all phases of the game, but you need a good start to have any hope of winning.

Research Capital Ship Drive.

Some players research Fighter or Corvette technologies first. But my advisors prefer to start with Capital Ship Drive. "It's the first step toward developing the big ships you need eventually," says QA tester Christopher Mason. "But even more important in the early going, it allows you to build Resource Controllers, which vastly improve the efficiency of your harvesting operation."

Start construction of another Research Ship.

Another no-brainer. You can't build a fleet without the technology to do so. The quicker you get the tech, the sooner you can outgun your opponents. Plus, every new Research Ship increases the survivability of your research operation because the new ship links to existing units, adding its armor rating to the aggregate armor of the entire research facility.

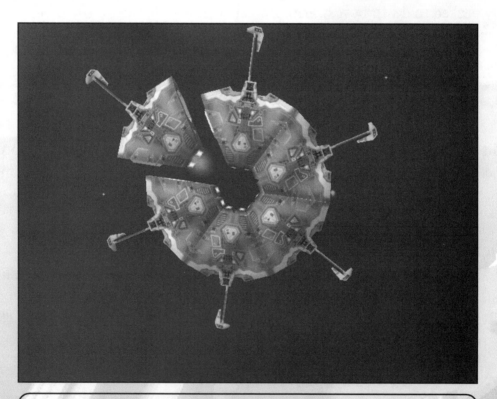

Fig. 2-2. Build multiple Research Ships to speed up crucial research and increase the facility's aggregate armor.

Never let a Research Ship sit idle!

This rule applies to any *Homeworld* scenario, but particularly to multiplayer games. *Keep a close eye on your Research activities!* Fleet Command prompts you whenever a technology research is done. But sometimes you're preoccupied with other tasks, or Fleet Command's voice gets lost in the general fleet chatter, so you don't hear the prompt. Better to rely on your own vigilance. Keep close tabs on any current research. The very moment one technology is ready, immediately start researching another.

Max out your Scout production.

Scouts are weak, but they're speedy. Best of all in the early going, they're cheap— only 35 RUs apiece. "I usually crank out the maximum number of Scouts right away," says Christopher Mason. "They aren't very tough ships, but they can defend your Collectors and Research Ships in the early phase of the game. At that point, nobody has anything better, usually."

NOTE

Don't worry too much about defending the Mothership in the early going. She's virtually impervious to enemy Scouts.

Harass the enemy's research facilities.

This tactic comes courtesy of QA tester Phil Kuhlmey. He says, "A last ditch trick is to send a bunch of Scouts to your enemy's Research Ship as soon as you can. If you can get there before the enemy has built a second Research Ship linked to the first one (which doubles the aggregate armor of the facility), then you can kamikaze your Fighters into the enemy Research Ship and BOOM! No more research."

Boy, that *is* low. But effective. Now your enemy has to spend several minutes building another Research Ship, which lets you get considerably ahead in the research department.

Build a Resource Controller *as soon as possible* and order it to "guard" Collectors.

Once Capital Ship Drive is researched, build a Resource Controller right away. If you assign a Controller to guard a single Resource Collector, the Controller sticks with the Collector, eliminating travel time. If you order the Controller to guard *two* Collectors, the Controller stays equidistant between the two designated Collectors. In either case, the Resource Controller greatly reduces that long slow trek between collection and deposit.

> ## NOTE
> Assign a stout group of Scouts—or later, Interceptors, Defenders, or Light Corvettes—to guard any Resource Controllers you build.

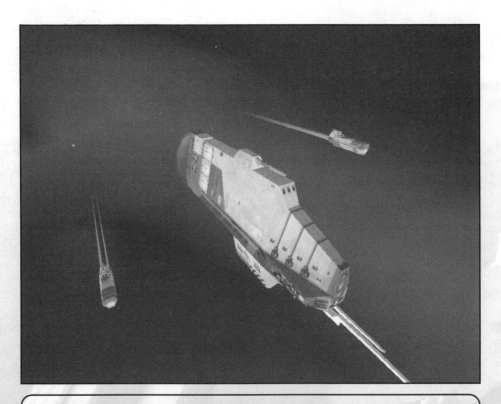

Fig. 2-3. Order your Resource Controller to "guard" one or two Collectors to speed up your harvesting operation.

Slightly favor resource collection over research in the early going.

But engage in both activities simultaneously. Our advice: Alternate construction of Resource Collectors and Research Ships until you have at least three of each. After that, Mason suggests, "give a slight nod toward building Collectors." After all, advanced research is useless without a sufficient store of RUs to build advanced craft. Remember that resources can be tapped out, so you should harvest as much as possible in the early and middle phases of the game.

Focus early research in either Fighter Systems or Corvette Systems, but not both.

In the early phase, getting to the higher technologies in either Fighter or Corvette Systems gives you a defense advantage over somebody who tries to develop both simultaneously. I'm a big fan of Defender Sub-Systems, because

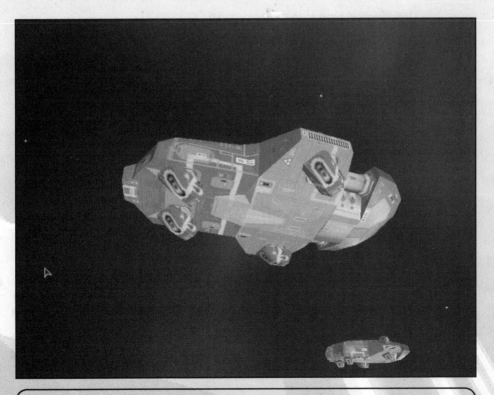

Fig. 2-4. The Multi-Gun Corvette, with its six fast-tracking turrets, is the best anti-Fighter craft in the game.

the Defender is tenaciously true to its name. As the game manual points out, "its gimbaled guns and high power rotational thrusters allow it the greatest coverage of all the Fighters." But Multi-Gun Corvettes are extremely effective against enemy Fighter swarms, as well.

Continue to research Capital Ship Systems, too.

After you get Capital Ship Drive technology, research Capital Ship Chassis. This technology lets you build Assault Frigates and also puts you just one technology step away from producing the core unit of your big-gun Battle Group—the Ion Cannon Frigate.

As Christopher Mason explains, "I like a few Assault Frigates in the early phase. But I build only four or five because they count against the same Frigate unit cap as Ion Cannon Frigates, and I want as many of those as possible." In other words, the more Assault Frigates you build now, the fewer Ion Cannon Frigates you can build later (unless, of course, you lose your Assault Frigates in battle or scrap them with the Retire command).

Middle Phase: Defend Supply Lines and Diversify the Fleet

OK, you've got at least three Research Ships developing technologies and three or four Resource Collectors sucking in the RUs. You've just acquired Ion Cannon technology; you're also equipped to build Corvettes or more advanced Fighters. Now it's time to diversify the fleet and assign beefier escorts to your vulnerable resourcing operations.

Crank out the Ion Cannon Frigates.

Yes, start building as many of these babies as you can. The Ion Cannon Frigate features the best bang for the buck *by far* at this point in the game. Sure, it's none too nimble, and its single gun is awfully slow to "reload." But check out its firepower rating; it packs a devastating punch.

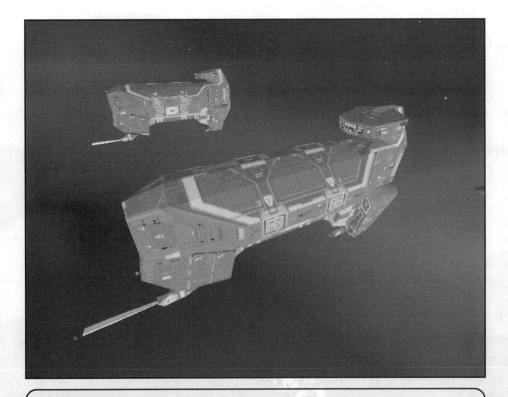

Fig. 2-5. The Ion Cannon Frigate is the basic unit of your primary attack fleet.

Your short-term goal is to build two groups of five apiece hovering about your Mothership, then add a few extra for raiding parties or a Resource Collector escort.

Focus research on Fighter or Corvette Systems, but don't ignore Capital Ship Systems.

Christopher Mason says, "After I get Ion Cannons, my development strategy can vary. If I don't feel much pressure from other players, I'll continue developing Capital System technologies—usually Super-Capital Ship Drive so I can build Destroyers. More often, though, I feel the need to get Strike Craft out to defend what by now should be a fairly large resourcing operation—at least four Resource Collectors with a Controller for every one or two Collectors."

If this is the case, Mason will research either Fighter Systems until he has Plasma Bomb Launcher technology (for Attack Bombers) or Corvette Systems to get Fast-Tracking Turrets (for Multi-Gun Corvettes). Allocate the majority of your Research Ships to this activity, but keep at least one dedicated to Capital Ship research.

Upgrade the protection for your Resource Collectors and Controllers.

With four or five Collectors and at least two Controllers out harvesting now, your resource operation is fanning out over an ever-widening area. You've probably already crossed paths with roving enemy units a few times as you compete for precious resources. Soon your Collectors will take heat from enemy marauders with firepower too hot for mere Scout escorts.

So it's time to beef up the guard. Heavy Corvettes or, better yet, Multi-Gun Corvettes (if available yet) make excellent escorts because of their anti-Fighter capability. Or if you focused your early research on Fighter Systems, assign a mix of Interceptors and Defenders—three of each is a good squad—to guard each Collector and Controller, putting the escort group in Sphere formation.

Eventually, as your enemies develop more powerful raiding parties, you may need to add a few Frigates (Assault or Ion Cannon) to your Resource Collector/Controller escort groups. But for now, in this middle phase of the game, advanced Fighters and Corvettes should keep your supply lines open.

> **TIP**
> Don't forget that Resource Controllers can refuel Strike Craft—up to six Fighters and two Corvettes at once via its docking pads.

Disrupt your enemy's resource collection activities.

Here's the converse of the previous tip. Some players love to raid harvesting operations; done properly, it can effectively sap your enemy's ability to fight. Three Ion Cannon Frigates guarded by five or six Multi-Gun Corvettes (or by a sphere of Defenders) make an excellent raiding party. This group will outgun most escorts assigned to guard enemy Resource Collectors. Another option: Replace the Frigates with a wing of Attack Bombers.

Start building your main Battle Group.

Ah, this is what you've been waiting for. After

> ### TIP
> Your best bet is to target enemy collection teams that meander farthest from their Mothership area. This tactic lets you hit and run before heavy reinforcements arrive. Focus all ion beams on the Collector and let your Corvettes deal with its Fighter escorts. One other tip: Add a Repair Corvette to your raiding group to refuel Fighters or Corvettes that run dry on their wide-ranging patrols.

all the asteroid digging and pointy-headed "research" and Scout skirmishes, it's finally time to prep a Battle Group that can slug it out with the big boys on the other side. You need enough firepower to survive Capital Ship combat and still knock out a Mothership.

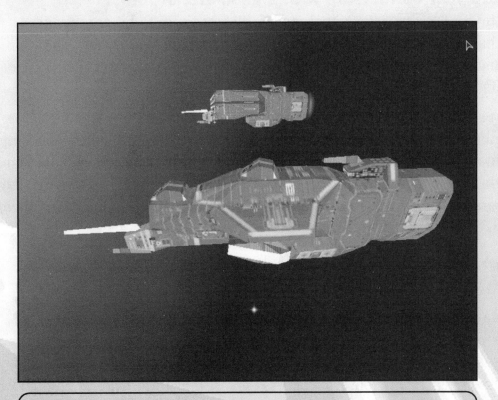

Fig. 2-6. The Destroyer (front) and its cousin, the Missile Destroyer (rear), are the power and the glory of any Battle Group.

Your Ion Cannon Frigates are a good start—you'll need at least 10 or 12, and preferably more. But the heart of your Battle Group is the mighty Destroyer. QA tester Erinn Hamilton recommends that you build at least two, then add three or four of the less powerful but more versatile Missile Destroyers.

Later, if time and RUs permit, you can add a Heavy Cruiser or two to the mix. But *Homeworld* multiplayer games sometimes move too fast to allow the resource accumulation necessary to build one of these lumbering behemoths.

Endgame Phase: The Mothership Rush

Enough sparring! Time to go toe to toe, fleet to fleet with the other guy(s). But before you commit your fledgling Battle Group to a power rush of enemy Motherships, you'd better secure your own base.

Guard your Mothership with a good mix of units.

Multiplayer veterans know that one of the best times to hit another player's Mothership is when he's trying to hit yours. So deploy a sizeable and well-balanced defense around your Mothership before you send your Battle Group on its attack run.

For Mothership defense, you need big gunships like the Ion Cannon Frigate to hurt attacking Capital Ships, plus plenty of Strike Craft to engage enemy Fighters and Attack Bombers. Plant a few Proximity Sensors nearby to detect cloaked vessels sneaking into the arena. Consider adding a few Gravity Well Generators, too. These can freeze enemy Strike Craft in place, making them sitting ducks for your defense guns.

(For more specific tips on how to assemble a defense group, see the Defending section in Chapter 1, General Tips.)

Guard your Battle Group against enemy Strike Craft.

One mistake many rookies make (if they last this long) is dumping *all* available resources into a Battle Group of big hulking Capital Ships. They deploy this seemingly invincible armada to hit an enemy Mothership…and then watch in anguish as Attack Bomber groups and other swarming Strike forces nibble their mighty Destroyers into space debris.

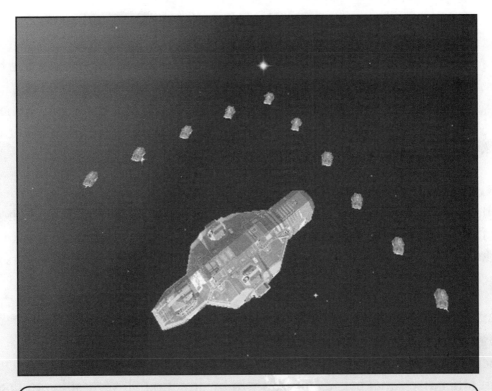

Fig. 2-7. Never ever send out a big, expensive capital ship without an escort of Strike Craft guarding it.

The obvious counter to such a scenario: Guard your Battle Group with Defenders and Multi-Gun Corvettes—or with what QA tester Christopher Mason calls "the poor man's defense,"—Interceptors and Heavy Corvettes. Note also that Missile Destroyers are much more effective against Strike Craft than other capital ships. Torsten Reinl, the QA lead, says, "I usually build at least four Missile Destroyers, using some for defense and some for offense. They give me quick and plentiful firepower against furballs of Strike Craft."

Carefully monitor enemy Battle Groups.

Probes are wonderful devices—cheap and expendable but so very valuable, particularly in the endgame phase. For a mere 30 RUs, you can zap a Probe into the heart of enemy space and see what your opponent's up to.

Keep a batch of five or so Probes handy at all times during the late stages of a game. Whenever your long-range sensors reveal a red blip moving toward your Mothership, immediately deploy a Probe for a closer look. Maybe the blip is just a Resource Collector and its escorts. Maybe it's an X-formation of Fighters roaming the supply routes. Then again, maybe it's the enemy's main Battle Group, making its final rush on your Mothership. Gosh, wouldn't it be nice to know for sure?

Destroy enemy Probes whenever possible.

And here's the converse of the previous tip. The less your enemy knows about your fleet deployment, the greater your advantage. Your Mothership sensors can detect and report Probes in the vicinity. Keep a small cluster of Scouts or Interceptors ready to pounce on any Probe that violates your near space.

When Battle Groups collide, concentrated fire brings the quickest knockouts.

"Concentrated fire is definitely the way to go," says QA tester Phil Kuhlmey. "In an otherwise equal battle, you can win by directing all your ships to take out individual enemy ships, one by one. If you select all your ships and then just use 'band-boxing' to target big bunches of enemy ships, you usually lose, unless your force is *considerably* stronger than theirs."

This is probably one of the most fundamental and effective fleet combat tips we can offer, so let me expand on it in detail. Sooner or later, your Battle Group is going to knock heads with an enemy Battle Group. Both sides will bring a *lot* of firepower to bear. Before you deploy your Battle Group, assign a single group number to *all* of your Capital Ships. (Keep any sub-groups assigned for flexible maneuvering.) Then put this mega-group into Wall formation and advance on the enemy. When you contact a hostile fleet, select your newly assigned Capital Ship mega-group and direct its total firepower at a single enemy Capital Ship. We suggest starting at the frigate level.

You will find that this "concentrated fire" method thins the enemy's ranks very, very quickly—much more quickly than by maneuvering your fleet into a bunch of individual ship-versus-ship exchanges. Indeed, your Battle Group's concentrated fire will pop open enemy frigates with a satisfying alacrity.

Fig. 2-8. Concentrate the fire of your entire Battle Group on one enemy Capital Ship at a time in any fleet-to-fleet engagement.

NOTE

Use the "move-attack" as well in Capital Ship combat. Order a Capital Ship to attack then get it moving. It will face its target as it moves, dealing unanswered damage!

Remember, once you destroy a target with concentrated fire, *immediately* select the next target. Your opponent may be using the same tactic against you. In this case, it becomes a race. The more efficient and alert your targeting, the better your chances of winning the engagement.

NOTE

If your Battle Group is **really** large—say, 30 or more capital ships—split it into two sub-groups of roughly equal firepower. Then assign group numbers to each sub-group for easy selection. This way you can hit **two** targets at once with enough firepower to make the "concentrated fire" tactic still effective.

Deploy (and beware of) Capture Groups.

QA Lead Torsten Reinl is fond of using Salvage Corvettes for sneaky capture tactics, particularly effective in the swirling confusion of a big fleet engagement. QA tester Erinn Hamilton suggests that you comprise your Capture Group of at least two Salvage Corvettes, four Cloak Generators, and 6-12 Light Corvettes for protection. Deploy the group in Wall formation, with a Cloak Generator activated. Then slip your invisible group up to enemy capital ships and "salvage" them—that is, steal them from under your enemy's nose.

Fig. 2-9. Salvage Corvettes hidden by a Cloak Generator can slip in and "steal" enemy ships. (Your cloaked ships appear in wireframe.)

Against more than one opponent, don't commit your Battle Group to an all-out offensive unless other sides are fighting each other, too.

This is just a bit of common sense. Certain failure awaits those who slog thigh-deep into mortal combat with one opponent, while other opponents sit back, harvest, build, and watch like vultures.

Attack the weakest available opponent.

Sure, it's despicable. But this is war. If your Probes reveal a weakened enemy—one decimated by a recent battle with another opponent, or perhaps one weakened by raids on his resource collection—go for the jugular.

Gang up on strong opponents.

Provisional alliances are a fact of life in multiplayer gaming. If you lose badly in a fleet-to-fleet engagement, or if your Probes detect an opponent with a particularly powerful fleet in the making—one you can't fight on your own—then consider forming alliances with other weak sides against the strong opponent.

Fight only one opponent at a time, if possible.

General war is inevitable, but try to manipulate the situation to isolate your enemies. Two-front conflicts are always costly and difficult to manage. Again, alliances can be very effective, in a Machiavellian sort of way. You know that sooner or later you'll have to crush your ally, but in the meantime you can work together to thin out the multiplayer map.

Once you reach an enemy Mothership, go for broke!

Concentrate your Battle Group's Capital Ship firepower, *every last ounce of it,* on the rival Mothership and let your Strike raft deal with her defenders. Frankly, this can be risky advice. It's not easy to train all big guns on a Mothership while her minions slice up your group, ship by ship. But remember, once the enemy Mothership is destroyed, its entire fleet is toast, too. You win.

This tip applies particularly to one-on-one games or to games where all other opponents have been defeated. Obviously, if you expend your fleet in a frontal assault but still have other enemies to face, you're in trouble. But let's face it. Sooner or later you have to slug it out with *someone* in a multiplayer game. Don't be hesitant or half-hearted. Go for it!

How to Adapt to Special Multiplayer Options

All of the tips in the previous section apply to standard multiplayer games. Of course, "standard" is a broad term that begins to lose meaning as you experiment more and more with special options. So we pose our next question to our panel of experts: "How do different scenarios affect the fleet you build?"

Short Games, Low Resources

QA lead Torsten Reinl says, "Short games with limited resources place more emphasis on smaller craft, which are cheaper and built in far less time than the super-Capital Ships." Indeed, when resources are scarce and the game is quick, building a Heavy Cruiser or even a Destroyer can be a waste of RUs and time.

QA tester Phil Kuhlmey agrees that the optimal fleet configuration is quite different if the game settings are very limited. "If I'm playing a Carrier-Only game, for example," he says, "I research and build Fighters (especially Defenders), then go straight for the quick kill before anyone can build Capital Ships."

NOTE

Something to think about: It's OK to play without injections. Fleet size will be limited, but this puts the focus on strategy and micro-management. Some players will find the depth of *Homeworld* play will vastly increase without injections.

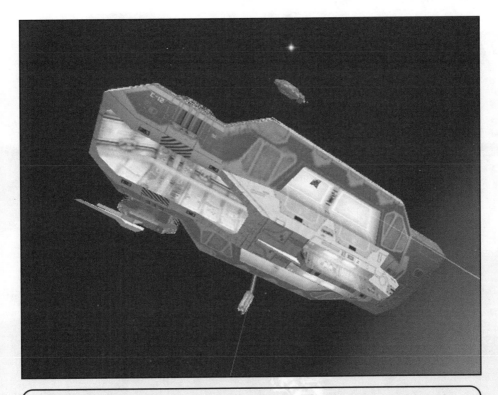

Fig. 2-10. In Carrier-Only scenarios, consider going for the quick kill using only Fighter groups.

Long Games, High Resources

On the other hand, if the game is long and resources are plentiful, it's almost the other way around. "If you have the time and money to build Missile Destroyers and Drone Frigates, Strike Craft don't last long in a full frontal assault," says Reinl. Instead, he uses Strike Craft for guard duty, for small harassing strikes, and for raiding enemy Resource Collectors.

"If it's a longer game on a bigger map," Reinl says, "I usually add a touch of sneakiness with Salvage Corvettes or Minelayer Corvettes." As mentioned earlier, one of Reinl's favorite tactics is to use Salvage Corvettes to nab enemy ships. He also likes to sow mines in rich resource areas. "There's nothing more upsetting than seeing half your fleet stolen from under your nose, or losing an entire resource operation to a gigantic minefield."

PART 2
SINGLE-PLAYER
MISSIONS

Thomas Wolfe said you can't go home again. But I don't think he had a Mothership. If you've skirmished the CPU, knocked heads with a few human opponents, and read the first two chapters of this book, you're ready for the challenge of following the Guidestone map back to Hiigara, your homeworld.

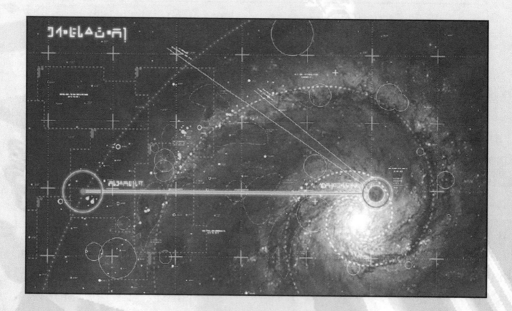

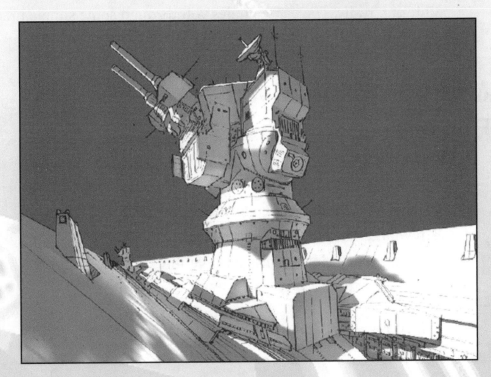

CHAPTER 3
THE KHARAK MISSIONS

MISSION 01: KHARAK SYSTEM

Here's a classic starter mission—more like an extension of the Training tutorial, really. The game guides you through some simple practice routines, so we won't add our own handholding here.

Mission Objectives
Primary

- Harvest asteroids.
- Construct a Research Ship.
- Destroy target drones using a formation.
- Destroy target drones using tactics.
- Capture a drone using a Salvage Corvette.

Secondary

- Research Fighter Chassis.

Research

- Fighter Chassis
- Corvette Drive

Fleet Construction

Start by building a Research Ship. When the game prompts you, build a Salvage Corvette for the salvage test. After you research Fighter Chassis technology, build a small wing (five or six) of Interceptors.

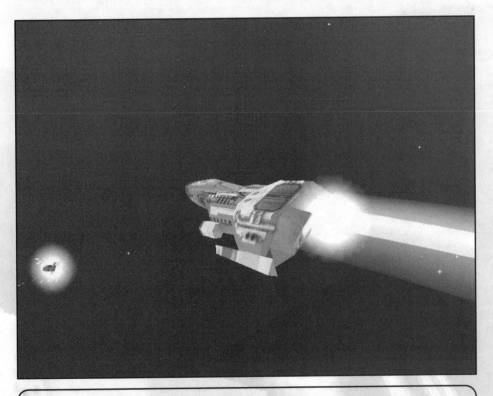

Fig. 3-1. What a bunch of drones. Wouldn't it be great if every space-faring enemy sat motionless in a parking lot?

Mission Strategy

This is a test, this is *only* a test. Simply follow Fleet Intelligence directives to fulfill the mission objectives. You'll make your first hyperspace test jump to a predetermined location on the outskirts of the Kharak system.

Fig. 3-2. The Mothership takes its first baby steps—and then one giant leap for humankind.

MISSION 02: OUTSKIRTS OF KHARAK SYSTEM

Congratulations! You executed your first hyperspace jump without extruding your molecular structure into a thin filament of subatomic particles.

The plan here is to hook up with a Kushan support vessel, the *Khar-Selim,* sent 10 years ago via conventional drive technology to these outskirts of the

Kharak system. Your primary goal is to monitor the effectiveness of your nascent hyperdrive technology. But when you arrive, the Support Vessel *Khar-Selim* is not responding. Sensors pick up the vessel's automated beacon about 55 kilometers from your arrival point.

Mission Objectives

Primary

- Send probe to the *Khar-Selim*.
- Defend the Mothership.
- Salvage the *Khar-Selim*.
- Defend salvage team.
- Destroy the attacking force.

Secondary

- Investigate power source (Carrier).

Research

- Corvette Chassis
- Heavy Corvette Upgrade

Fleet Construction

You need strong wings of Fighters for both attack and escort duty in this mission; add enough Interceptors for two groups of eight. After you research Corvette technologies, you can and should build four Heavy Corvettes. This mission throws an ugly swarm of hostile Fighters and Corvettes at you, and Heavy Corvettes provide a strong defense against such attacks.

Also, build a Probe to send to the *Khar-Selim* beacon.

You can't complete this mission without a Salvage Corvette to retrieve the *Khar-Selim*'s mission data recorder. You built one in the last mission; if you play intelligently, you won't need another one here. However, consider building at least five more Salvage Corvettes (for a total of six) at the end of this mission, before you make your next hyper-space jump. You'll need them for Mission 03, "Return to Kharak."

> **TIP**
>
> Be patient! Don't investigate the *Khar-Selim* beacon until you've harvested all area resources, researched all available Corvette Class technologies, and built at least three Heavy Corvettes and 10 Interceptors.

Mission Strategy

Your first big *Homeworld* surprise lurks near the *Khar-Selim*. But it won't manifest itself until you investigate, so don't hurry to trigger its appearance. First, direct your lone Resource Collector to start harvesting; few resources exist in this empty region, so you don't need additional Collectors yet. Also, start researching the Corvette Chassis technology. Completing that allows you to research the Heavy Corvette Upgrade; do so as soon as you can.

> **TIP**
>
> Use the Sensors Manager to keep an eye on your Resource Collector. Don't let it wander near the **Khar-Selim**! If it does, it will trigger the enemy ambush before you're ready.

Of course, the young and the reckless may want to rush out to that pulsing *Khar-Selim* beacon. Again, consider completing *all* resource collection and *all* available research before you approach the beacon.

Build enough Interceptors for two groups of eight, and then add four Heavy Corvettes. (You must wait until your Resource Collector brings in additional harvest loads.)

Designate the Heavy Corvettes "Group 1" for easy ID, and then deploy in a Sphere formation to defend your Research Ship. Designate your Interceptors "Group 2" and "Group 3," each in a Claw, and position them near the Research Ship, as well. Don't worry about the Mothership in this scenario; she can handle herself.

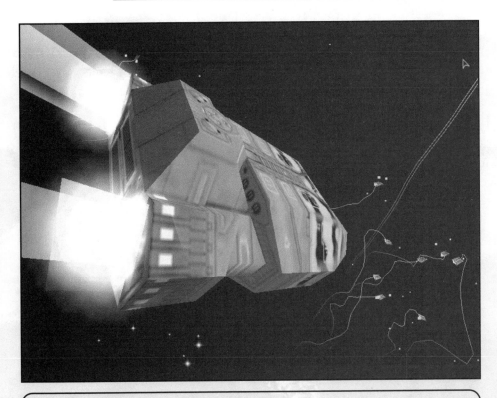

Fig. 3-3. Don't investigate the **Khar-Selim** beacon until you're ready. Any approach triggers a vicious enemy ambush of Fighters and Corvettes.

Designate your small group of Scouts "Group 4" and assign it to guard your Salvage Corvette. Move the Corvette to a safe distance (at least a kilometer) from the Mothership. Now build a Probe and send it to the *Khar-Selim* beacon (the yellow blip on the Sensors Manager screen).

When the Probe reaches the *Khar-Selim,* things happen fast, but now you're prepared. A sudden wave of hostile Fighters and Corvettes ambushes your base area. Some focus on the Mothership, but your Research Ship is a more vulnerable target, so guard it well. Your Heavy Corvettes provide a sturdy defense as you direct your Interceptor groups to pounce on targets one at a time.

After you destroy the first enemy wave, send your Salvage Corvette to retrieve the *Khar-Selim*'s mission data recorder. But make sure it's well-escorted. Assign groups 1 and 2 (Heavy Corvettes and Interceptors) to defend the salvage vessel in Sphere formations.

When the Salvage Corvette reaches the Support Vessel *Khar-Selim*, direct it to salvage the main compartment. More hostile units soon try to disrupt this operation, but your escort group should be strong enough to knock out each enemy wave during the trek back to the Mothership.

When the Salvage Corvette returns to the Mothership with the mission recorder, review the tragic *Khar-Selim* mission data. Then more waves of enemy craft hit your base area—again, Corvettes as well as Fighters.

Fig. 3-4. Don't chase the enemy Carrier! It's suicide for your current fleet.

As Fleet Intelligence points out, your forces are superior, so you should win easily. But when FC detects a "large power signature" nearby, send a Scout to investigate. (Again, look for the yellow blip on the Sensor screen.) You'll find a massive enemy Carrier. Don't attack it! You'll suffer big losses to no avail. Fortunately, the Carrier soon realizes defeat and starts recalling its attack wings. When that happens, you've won.

Mission 03, "Return to Kharak," starts with a bang, so do a little ship-building and make a quick organization check before you jump into hyper-space. Your Heavy Corvettes are Group 1, and your Interceptors are groups 2 and 3. Build five more Salvage Corvettes for a total of six, and then assign them a group number.

Finally, execute your hyperspace jump back to Kharak orbit.

Fig. 3-5. Create a group of at least six Salvage Corvettes **before** you make the hyperspace jump back to Kharak orbit.

MISSION 03: RETURN TO KHARAK

Here's your first truly challenging mission. Not only must you battle superior enemy craft—a five-pack of Assault Frigates—but you must capture and salvage at least one of them (all five, if possible). This makes for some tricky combat maneuvers.

Fig. 3-6. Kharak burns, low orbit's a mess, and five big Assault Frigates blast your Cryo Trays. Capture them!

Mission Objectives

- Defend Cryo Trays.
- Capture enemy ship using two Salvage Corvettes.
- Salvage Cryo Trays.

Research

- Capital Ship Drive (after capturing one enemy Assault Frigate)
- Capital Ship Chassis

Fleet Construction

After you gain Capital Ship Drive technology and the skirmish is over, build a Resource Controller and a second Resource Collector.

Mission Strategy

Your return to Kharak is a shocker: the planet is burning and low Kharak orbit is a floating junkyard. To make matters worse, enemy Assault Frigates open fire on your defenseless Cryo Trays almost immediately upon your return. If your fleet is insufficient to deploy now—particularly the six Salvage Corvettes—you have precious little time to build what you need.

First, send your speedy Interceptors to "group attack" (drag an attack box around) the enemy Frigates. Quickly do the same with your Heavy Corvette group. As the battle rages, slip your Salvage Corvettes quietly onto the scene.

Your goal here is to "salvage"—that is, capture—as many hostile Assault Frigates as you can while protecting your Cryo Trays from complete destruction. Your mission objectives require you to salvage only one Frigate, but each extra one you snatch adds that ship to your own fleet.

> # NOTE
> You need two Salvage Corvettes to retrieve each big Assault Frigate. But if you can lock on with one Salvage Corvette, the tug will spin the Frigate, disrupting its firing pattern and maneuverability.

Fig. 3-7. Harass the Assault Frigates with your Strike groups as you sneak in your Salvage Corvettes from behind.

It's very difficult to capture all five enemy Capital Ships. One reason—when a Salvage Corvette latches onto a Frigate, the other Frigates attempt (with deadly accuracy and single-mindedness) to shoot the tug off their brother's back. To protect your Salvage Corvettes, harass and draw enemy fire with your Strike craft groups. In the process, your Fighters may destroy a Frigate or two. Just remember, if you destroy *all five* enemy Assault Frigates, you fail the mission.

Once one enemy Frigate is safely stowed aboard the Mothership, a mission data recording displays the destruction of Kharak. You also "reverse engineer" Capital Ship Drive technology—that is, you gain it automatically. Continue attempting to capture the remaining enemy Assault Frigates. If your Salvage Corvettes capture the final enemy ship, call off your Strike craft groups' attack immediately.

To complete your mission objectives, send your Salvage Corvettes to pull in the remaining Cryo Trays. (You'll need only one tug per tray.) Order your Resource Collector to begin harvesting. Then begin research on Capital Ship Chassis.

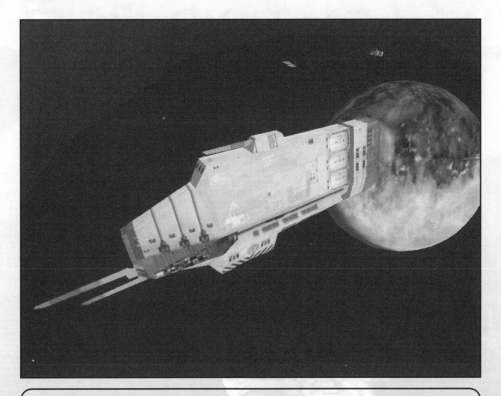

Fig. 3-8. Save enough RUs to build a Resource Controller before you jump to the next mission.

After completing all research and harvesting the meager local resources, consider building a newly available Resource Controller: your next mission takes place in a resource-rich asteroid belt.

Now you can initiate your hyperspace jump to the "Great Wastelands."

Chapter 4
The Asteroid Belt Missions

The next three missions take place in an asteroid-filled region largely void of settled life, but rich in resources. Here, in the Great Wastelands, you conduct your first trade with the ancient Bentusi, encounter vicious pirates, and finally engage the brutal Taiidan fleet that devastated Kharak.

Mission 04: Great Wastelands

This mission introduces you to a valuable trading partner, the Bentusi. These ancient merchants will be a source of valuable technology upgrades as you trek across the galaxy to Hiigara. Also, you face your first heavy-hitting Capital Ships—deadly Ion Array Frigates and a pirate Carrier.

Mission Objectives

- Begin collecting resources.
- Build and deploy Resource Controller.
- Protect the fleet from Turanic Raiders.
- Destroy retreating Turanic Raider Carrier.

Research

- Ion Cannons

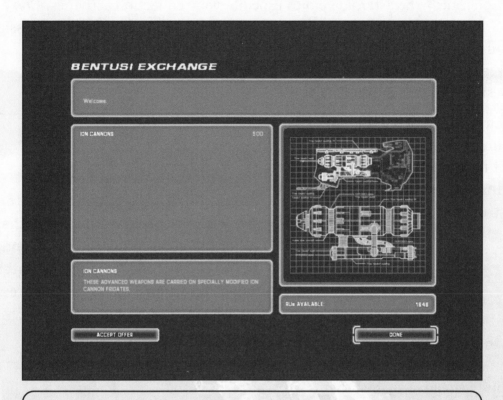

Fig. 4-1. Bentusi traders offer you Ion Cannon technology for a mere 300-500 RUs early in this scenario. Take the deal! It's a bargain.

Fleet Construction

If you didn't build a Resource Controller in the last mission, do so right away. Also, build enough Interceptors for two groups of eight, enough Heavy Corvettes for two groups of five, and, most important, enough Salvage Corvettes for three groups of three.

After the Bentusi sell you Ion Cannon technology, construct at least two Ion Cannon Frigates right away (if you have the RUs). (Your Salvage Corvettes should capture most of the enemy's Ion Array Frigates, as well.) You'll need the ion beam firepower to knock out the Turanic Raider Carrier.

Mission Strategy

When you arrive, Fleet Intelligence suggests you position a Resource Controller near the asteroid vein to expedite your collection activities. *Don't do this.* Instead, order your Controller to "guard" your Resource Collector. Assign a group of Heavy Corvettes (at least five, if you can) and about half your Interceptors to defend the Controller. Then order your Collector to start harvesting the rich asteroid belt.

You have no competition for the resources in this region, so you won't need a second Collector yet. Instead, *immediately* start constructing enough Salvage Corvettes to create three groups of three. Then add a second group of Heavy Corvettes, as many as you can afford, and order it to guard your Research Ship. You'll face thick Fighter swarms later in the mission, and Heavy Corvettes are quite effective against them.

TIP

Split your Salvage Corvettes into three groups of three. Send two groups 14 kilometers behind and to the left of the Mothership. Send the other the same distance behind and to the right of the Mothership. Later, when the Turanic Ion Array Frigates arrive, you'll be well-positioned for an easier capture.

Suddenly, Fleet Intelligence reports a "Mothership-class mass signature"—with off-the-scale power readings—closing fast on your position. Fortunately, the huge alien craft is a trading vessel, home of the Bentusi, who welcome you among the space-faring cultures they call "the Unbound." The traders report that the resource units you gather will serve as an acceptable medium for the Bentusi Trade Exchange.

NOTE

If you don't have enough RUs available to trade for Ion Cannon technology, just wait. Your Collector will deliver a load soon. When this happens, quickly select "Accept Offer."

The Bentusi equip their trading partners with an "exchange unit," and they offer one to you as a gesture of good will. Once your ambassador returns, the Bentusi Exchange

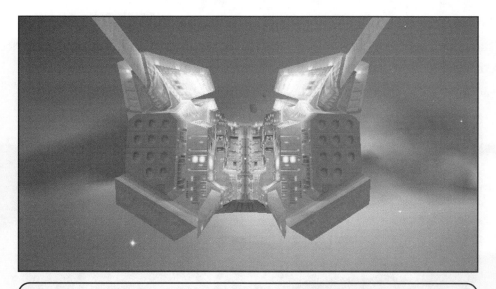

Fig. 4-2. Meet the Bentusi. They seem like nice guys. Take every trade they offer.

trading link appears onscreen automatically. The Bentusi offer you Ion Cannon technology for a measly 300-500 RUs. Don't hesitate to take the deal. Without Ion Cannons, your fleet will be at the mercy of enemy Capital Ships.

After you make the trade, the Bentusi warn you of approaching Turanic Raiders, servants of the Taiidan. Then the traders depart, saying they will "listen for you" in the void; that is, they'll return with other trade offers.

Important: *immediately* start constructing Ion Cannon Frigates! Build at least two. Enemy Capital Ships attack soon, and without a few Ion Cannon Frigates working in your defense, you face a difficult task.

The Turanic Raiders arrive: first, a swarm of Fighters and a few Missile Corvettes attack your harvesting operation. The stout escort of Heavy Corvettes and Interceptors should defend your Resource Controller effectively, but send more if things get dicey.

Soon after, four powerful Ion Array Frigates hyperspace onto the scene and advance on your Mothership with their devastating ion beams. This is the trickiest (and most fun) part of this mission. Direct each group of three Salvage

Corvettes to capture an enemy Frigate. Fire on the fourth Frigate with any combat craft you have available. The Frigates will turn immediately to target approaching Corvettes, and you'll likely lose one in each group. But the surviving two should have time to latch onto their salvage targets.

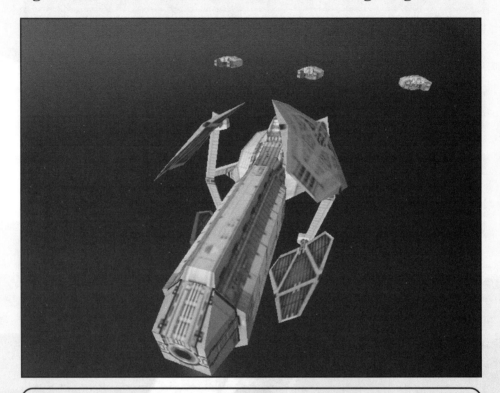

Fig. 4-3. Try to steal three of the four Ion Array Frigates that hit early. Best bet—deploy three Salvage Corvettes toward each one.

Three free Ion Array Frigates! Wow. Not even the Bentusi can beat that deal.

Finally, a massive Turanic Carrier escorted by two more Ion Array Frigates slides in to attack your Mothership. Direct your full ion cannon force (those you built, plus those you captured) to attack the Carrier; then deploy Salvage Corvettes to capture both escorting enemy Frigates. Once you snag the Frigates, you can turn your full attention to the Carrier, which tries to escape. Don't let it! Hit it with every gun you've got.

After you destroy the Carrier, finish up harvesting in the area and then hyperspace to your next jump point.

MISSION 05: GREAT WASTELANDS

Get ready for your first taste of serious fleet-to-fleet combat. The genocidal Taiidan force, instrument of your planet's destruction, lurks just beyond the heavy dust clouds of the Wastelands. When you arrive, you're not yet ready to wreak your revenge. Fortunately, the area's rich resource deposits will fill your RU banks and let you build a fledgling Battle Group.

Mission Objectives

Primary

- Investigate the asteroid belt.
- Eradicate all enemy ships.

Secondary

- Destroy enemy Resource Collectors.
- Research Defender Subsystems.

Research

- Plasma Bomb Launcher
- Defender Subsystems

Fleet Construction

Time to beef up a bit. You need a Battle Group of at least 10 Ion Cannon Frigates/Ion Array Frigates to tangle with the Taiidan Capital Ships in this mission, which include a Carrier and a pair of Destroyers. You also need sufficient Strike craft to defend the Battle Group against the dozens of Fighters the enemy Carrier deploys. Be sure you have at least 10-12 Heavy Corvettes and a couple of groups of 10 Interceptors—and more if at all possible.

After you destroy the Taiidan fleet, build a single group of 30 Fighters—15 Attack Bombers and 15 Defenders—to prepare for the next mission.

Mission Strategy

First, ignore Fleet Intelligence's suggestion to send a Probe to investigate the Taiidan position beyond the dust clouds—for now, anyway. However, do send a Probe 49 kilometers from the Mothership directly toward the yellow ping on your sensors. This gives you a 49-kilometer mark on your Sensors Manager. (See Figure 4-4.) If any of your ships cross this mark, you trigger the Taiidan's full assault. You don't want to fight just yet.

Instead, start harvesting. Be sure to assign a strong escort of Strike craft (Heavy Corvettes and Interceptors) to the Controller of this harvesting group. *Don't let your harvesters wander beyond that 49-kilometer mark!* Open your Sensors Manager, rotate the map to Overhead view, and note how the resource-laden dust clouds form a 'V' shape opening toward your Mothership. Your Collectors start working their way up one stem of the vee toward the Taiidan

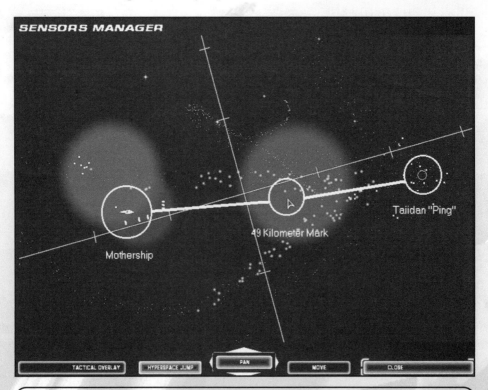

Fig. 4-4. Send a Probe to this position, 49 kilometers from the Mothership. Don't let your ships wander past this mark until you're ready, or you'll trigger the Taiidan assault.

position. Keep an eye on them! When they get close to the 49-kilometer mark, order the Collectors to move back to the tip of the other stem of the vee. This lets you harvest the maximum amount of resources—and thus maximize your fleet construction—before you must face the Taiidan assault.

As you harvest, build your fleet steadily. You need a Battle Group of at least 10 Ion Cannon Frigates (including the captured Ion Array Frigates) and plenty of Interceptors and Heavy Corvettes to escort them. Don't hold back. Build the biggest fleet possible, until the resources run dry on your side of the 49-kilometer mark.

The Taiidan forces are formidable, but they move forward piecemeal. Pull your entire harvesting operation back near the Mothership for now. You can harvest at your leisure after you win the battle.

Meanwhile, move your Battle Group in Wall formation straight up the middle of the vee, toward the yellow blip on your Sensor screen. A wave of

Fig. 4-5. Assemble a Battle Group of ion-cannon-equipped Capital Ships and send it forward in Wall formation.

three Assault Frigates comes at you first, followed closely by a second, identical, wave. These should provide a light lunch for your wall of ion-beam Capital Ships, as long as you concentrate fire on them one at a time.

Stay sharp! A trio of Taiidan Ion Cannon Frigates soon slides in below the Assault Frigate waves. These dish out more damage, but you have them outnumbered at least 3 to 1. When they hit your Battle Group, turn your full attention to them and leave any remaining Assault Frigates for later.

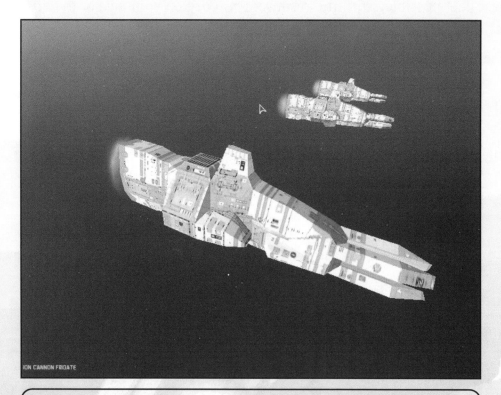

ION CANNON FRIGATE

Fig. 4-6. Concentrate on the arriving enemy Ion Cannon Frigates and ignore any remaining Assault Frigates for now.

Next comes a fearsome sight: two powerful Taiidan Destroyers, guns thundering. Concentrate fire on one at a time. If one slips away, just let it go for now. A single Assault Frigate with an escort of new Defenders soon follows. As you blast this lone duck, start researching your own Defender Subsystems technology. Finally, you'll encounter the source of all those pesky enemy

Fighters—a Taiidan Carrier with a Support Frigate to repair and refuel the Strike craft. Lay into the Carrier with 10 ion guns blazing. It takes time to kill it, but when a Carrier goes, it goes beautifully. Knock out the Support Frigate too, then send your Battle Group hustling back home.

Why? Those enemy Probes you've heard Fleet Intelligence reporting have pinpointed your Mothership, drawing the attention of the Taiidan Destroyer you let slip past. You still have it vastly outgunned, but look—it's making a run at your base. If you don't engage it first, it may take out your Research Ship and anything else parked near the Mothership.

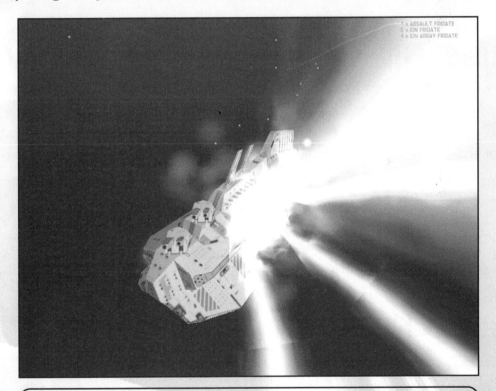

Fig. 4-7. This Taiidan Destroyer is a prize worth having. Try to capture it rather than blast it (like I'm doing here); you'll need three Salvage Corvettes to haul it in.

So catch up and kill it. Or, better yet, *snatch* it. It takes three Salvage Corvettes to haul in a Destroyer, but if you can pick off the Destroyer's escort Fighters, you stand a good chance of capturing the big boat. Just swarm it with a small group of Strike craft to draw fire away from the Salvage Corvettes.

After you capture or obliterate the Destroyer, you win. Hunt down the two enemy Resource Collectors at your leisure. (If you don't, they kamikaze right into the Mothership!) Now you have all the time in the world to research Plasma Bomb technology and harvest every last dustball in the region. Meanwhile, build a big batch of Strike craft for the next mission—ideally, a single group of 30 (15 Attack Bombers and 15 Defenders). Then assign one group number to *all* other ships combined, Capital and otherwise, except for your Resource Collectors. You'll see why in the next mission.

Jump to hyperspace.

MISSION 06: DIAMOND SHOALS

This mission may seem like a breather after the Taiidan engagement in the Great Wasteland, but don't be fooled. You emerge from hyperspace into the tail end of a turbulent asteroid field. Asteroids are big and slow, but so is your Mothership, and you must protect it at all costs. Keep in mind that asteroids can wreak havoc on the less nimble elements of your fleet, as well.

Mission Objectives

- Protect the Mothership.

Research

- Super–Capital Ship Drive
- Drone Technology (from the Bentusi)

Fleet Construction

If you didn't build up a contingent of at least 15 Attack Bombers and 15 Defenders at the end of the last mission, it may be too late to do so now. These nimble Strike craft are perfect for asteroid-bashing. Grouped as suggested, they have enough firepower to disintegrate rocks, and they're maneuverable enough to avoid getting smashed in the process.

Mission Strategy

Strategy for this mission is as simple as it gets in *Homeworld*. But that doesn't mean it's *easy*.

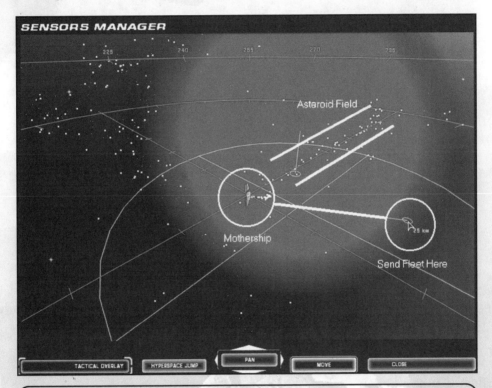

Fig. 4-8. Move the bulk of your fleet out and away from your Mothership to avoid asteroid casualties.

First, immediately move all your slower ships—Frigates, Corvettes, Resource Controller (but not Collectors), even your Research Ship—50 or so kilometers to the right and below your Mothership. (This task is easier if you assigned a single group number to these ships at the end of the last mission.) This deploys them safely out of the asteroid field. If you use Frigates to clear the field, you'll probably lose a few.

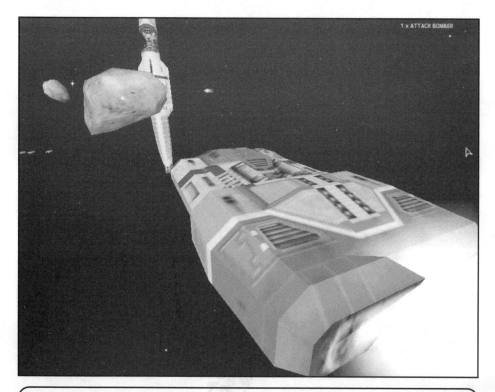

Fig. 4-9. Deploy nimble (and deadly) Attack Bombers and Defenders in a single group. Asteroids "melt" fast if you concentrate the group's full firepower on them one at a time.

Second, quickly order your Resource Collectors to start harvesting. They'll calmly gather several loads of RUs during the ensuing rock-dodging, rock-blasting madness.

Third, group all your Attack Bombers and Defenders together in Wall formation just ahead of your Mothership and start shooting rocks. If you have 30 or more of these Fighters in the wall, even the bigger asteroids "melt" quickly. Plus, your Strike craft are mobile enough to dodge rocks and still move from target to target quickly.

Note that all asteroids in the field approach from dead ahead. Most will miss the Mothership, so don't waste time and firepower on them. Instead, use your 3-D view to pinpoint actual threats.

> ### TIP
> Select the Mothership and press F to focus on her; then use the left mouse button to swing the camera above and slightly behind her. This way you can identify rocks looming dangerously in the collision envelope directly ahead of the Mothership. (See Fig. 4-10.)

In the midst of this rocking fun, recall that your Research Division is now equipped for Super–Capital Ship Drive technology. Start researching that when you have a break between asteroids.

After you clear the asteroid field, the Bentusi return offering a new trade—Drone Technology for 500 RUs. *Sold!* When you ask for advice on getting through the heart of the nebula ahead, the Bentusi intone ominously: "We hear nothing there. Even the Taiidan fear the Great Nebula. No one returns."

Excellent! Your species loves a challenge. *Hyperspace ho!*

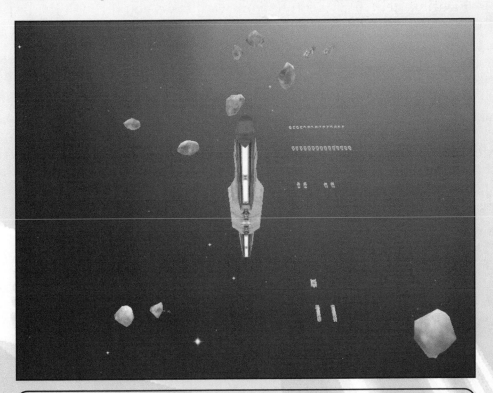

Fig. 4-10. Swing the 3-D camera to this view from behind the Mothership to spot dangerous rocks.

CHAPTER 5
THE GREAT NEBULA
MISSIONS

Tackling the first pair in this three-pack of missions is like taking Fighting Hell 101. Your trek homeward takes you through the heart of the Great Nebula's dense energy field. The guys in your harvesters are happy, but your arrival in the Garden of Kadesh prompts a little visit from its gardeners—a paranoid species of wayfarers who see the nebula as a holy place. And guess what: you defile it with your presence. You are unclean. And there is no withdrawal from the Garden.

The third mission jumps you to the outer fringe of the nebula and provides a bit of a breather...but only if you play it right. If you don't, the "Sea of Lost Souls" is a ghostly nightmare.

MISSION 07:
THE GARDENS OF KADESH

Here's a real donnybrook. The Bentusi said of the Great Nebula, "No one returns." Now you'll learn why. Your attempt to harvest resources in this sensor-warping energy field triggers the wrath of an odd, unnamed race cruising around in space-needle Motherships. They don't like you messing up their garden.

Mission Objectives

Primary

- Harvest the nebula.
- Defend the fleet.

Secondary

- Protect your resourcers.

Research

- Fast-tracking Turrets

Fleet Construction

First, retire any Attack Bombers left from the previous mission. They're too vulnerable against the agile "Swarmers" (amazingly quick little Fighters) you face in this mission. Then assemble the 35–45 Defenders and 18–24 Heavy Corvettes you'll need to survive this Mother of All Furballs.

The Drone Frigate can release a deadly sphere of 24 highly maneuverable drones that can decimate enemy Fighter swarms. Consider building one early—if you can afford it—to guard your most valuable Capital Ship (such as the Destroyer you may have captured in Mission 05). Again, this mission pits your fleet against an insane number of Fighters.

Early in the mission, Fleet Intelligence reports that your Research Division is ready to develop special anti-Fighter technology. Immediately research Fast-tracking Turrets and build a group of Multi–Gun Corvettes. Assemble as many of these ultimate Fighter-killers as you can.

Mission Strategy

The key to this mission can be summed up in four words: *Kill the Fuel Pods.*
Without their support pods, the enemy Swarmers quickly run dry and
remain stuck in position like flies on flypaper. Devote at least two groups of
12–15 Defenders to full-time pod-killing duty.

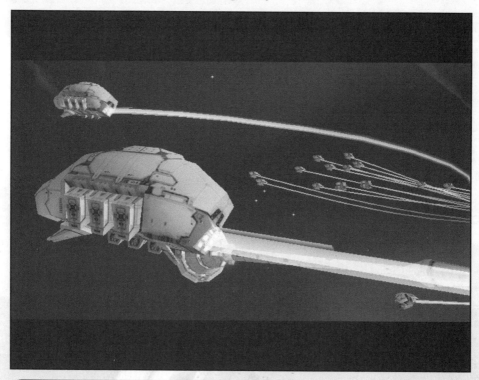

Fig. 5-1. Target slow-moving Fuel Pods with your Fighters and Capital
Ships. Without pods, Swarmers soon run dry and float like bubbles ready
to be popped.

One other important four-word tip to remember in the Gardens: *Ignore
the Needle Mothership*—until late in the mission, anyway. Do *not,* under any
circumstances, send your valuable Capital Ships after the enemy Mothership.
You can't kill her; she simply hops into hyperspace when hurt. (As Sierra QA
Tester "Nautikus" reports, "Some Needle Motherships ram right through your
Capital Ship formation if they get a chance. I've lost nine Ion Cannon Frigates
in one blow!")

Overall, your first goal is to survive for 10 minutes, until your hyperspace module has recharged fully. If you have the proper forces—*lots* of Defenders and Heavy Corvettes—this shouldn't be difficult. Your Mothership won't suffer much damage from the Swarmers and Advanced Swarmers that, well, *swarm* your position.

However, your expensive Capital Ships can get nibbled to death by the buzzing swarms. As you target Fuel Pods with your Fighter groups, then, be sure to throw up a hefty escort screen of Heavy Corvettes around your Battle Group, too.

> **TIP**
>
> Your Ion Cannon Frigates aren't entirely useless in this mission. True, they can't hit active Swarmers. But by all means use your Capital Ships to target the relatively immobile Fuel Pods or those clusters of Swarmers floating helplessly with spent fuel tanks.

At some point in the battle, the enemy's Needle Mothership will float past your own Mothership. Don't take the bait! Again, you can't destroy it; you'll simply lose ships needlessly in any assault. Continue to focus on Fuel Pods and Swarmers until Fleet Command announces your hyperdrive is ready to roll.

When your hyperdrive is ready, fire it up. But now you get a surprise. The jump fails! As Fleet Command reports, "The quantum waveform collapsed due to some kind of inhibitor field." Guess what's causing the inhibitor field? Yep, the Needle Mothership, which reappears and sends more Swarmers with Fuel Pods at you. Send a couple of Defender groups toward the enemy Mothership. After you damage her a bit (it doesn't take long), she disappears for good. Fleet Intelligence notes that the inhibitor field has disappeared. Finally, you're able to jump away.

But don't jump yet! Remember, this nebula is rich in resources. Kill off any remaining Swarmers and Fuel Pods, and then simply hang out until your resourcers suck the region dry.

Fig. 5-2. Add a strong contingent of Multi-Gun Corvettes before you jump to the next mission.

Meanwhile, build as many Strike craft as you can, because you won't have time to do so at the beginning of the next mission. Now that Multi–Gun Corvettes are available, retire all (yes, *all*) your Heavy Corvettes for the extra RUs. Your minimum fleet—three groups of 15 Defenders, two groups of 12 Multi–Gun Corvettes, and a strong Battle Group of 10 or more Ion Cannon Frigates (or the equivalent). Again, this is the *minimum* requirement for the next mission. Build more Fighters and Multi–Gun Corvettes if you have the funds.

Now jump to hyperspace. If you thought this mission was hectic...

MISSION 08: THE CATHEDRAL OF KADESH

Yes, it's a trap! This mission's brutal war of attrition will drain your fleet resources. In fact, a serious degradation of your Battle Group and Strike craft wings is almost unavoidable. And unlike in the previous mission, the Garden enemy deploys deadly Multi–Beam Frigates with more than sufficient firepower to knock out your Mothership.

Fortunately, the area is loaded with resources, so if you can survive the Cathedral's maniacal melee, you can rebuild afterward.

Mission Objectives

- Destroy the attackers.
- Destroy hyperspace inhibitors (three Needle Motherships).

Research

Sorry, no upgrades available this mission.

Fleet Construction

You should have built at least 45 Defenders and 24 Multi–Gun Corvettes at the end of the previous mission (Mission 07, "Gardens of Kadesh"). If you didn't, you may not last long here. You should also have a strong Battle Group of at least 10 Ion Cannon Frigates (or the equivalent).

If you lose your existing harvesters during this battle, build a new group after the mayhem ends. You need a Resource Collector (two, to save time) guarded by a Resource Controller to mine this region's rich resource deposits.

Mission Strategy

As Fleet Intelligence reports, you must destroy the three hyperspace inhibitors—again, Needle Motherships—that pulled you back into the nebula. But if you rush out after them, your Mothership is toast. Not from the Swarmers that hit you first; those are easily handled (as in the previous mission) by targeting their Fuel Pods. This time, the Garden's forces slip in eight spinning spheroids of death known as Multi–Beam Frigates.

These diabolical craft look like more Fuel Pods when they first approach, so it's easy to dismiss them—until they start their spinning attack. Each unleashes quad-ion beams, each Frigate packing enough heat to *single-handedly* fry your Mothership in about two minutes.

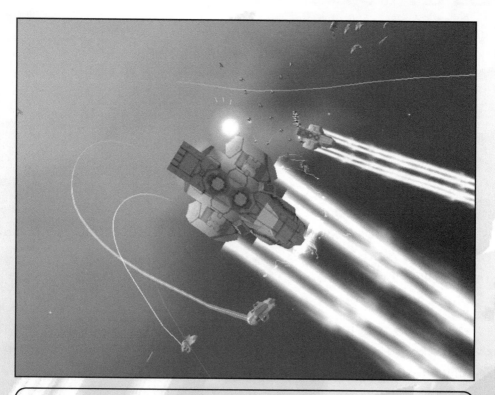

Fig. 5-3. These quad-firing Multi-Beam Frigates will take out your Mothership in less than a minute if you don't target them immediately.

Keep all Strike craft *and* your Battle Group at home. The Multi–Beam Frigates attack in four pairs. About a minute after the mission begins, the first pair approaches your Mothership from dead ahead. Soon another pair attacks from the Mothership's right. One option: Split your Battle Group into two units and send one at each of these first two Frigate pairs. A better option: Sic your Salvage Corvettes on them. Multi-Beam Frigates are fairly easy to capture because, despite all that power, they have lousy aim.

TIP

Capture as many Multi-Beam Frigates with your Salvage Corvettes as you can. These Frigates are excellent Mothership killers and will prove quite useful to you in this mission.

TIP

Consummate multitaskers should take a few split seconds (as they're fending off Swarmers and multiple Multi-Beam Frigates) to send your harvesters about 20 kilometers to the right of the Mothership. This usually moves them safely out of the crossfire.

Of course, while you're preoccupied, a third pair of Multi–Beam Frigates drops in quietly from above on the left side of your Mothership (which may be smoking and seriously damaged by now). If your Salvage Corvettes are still tied up, target this pair with your Capital Ships. (Keep your Defenders and Multi–Gun Frigates fighting the enemy Swarmers.) The fourth and final pair slips in quietly from the front. You must capture or eliminate all Multi–Beam Frigates as quickly as you can!

Once all eight Multi–Beam Frigates are added to your Battle Group or eliminated, go back to igniting Fuel Pods and clearing Swarmers from around the Mothership. When the area is secured, send your entire Battle Group, with *plenty* of escorts, to the nearest "inhibitor" (Needle Mothership) location. (It sits about 20 kilometers directly in front and above of your own Mothership.) Leave only a small defense group of Multi–Gun Corvettes with the Mothership. (Nothing other than a few Swarmers will attack her, if you play your cards right.)

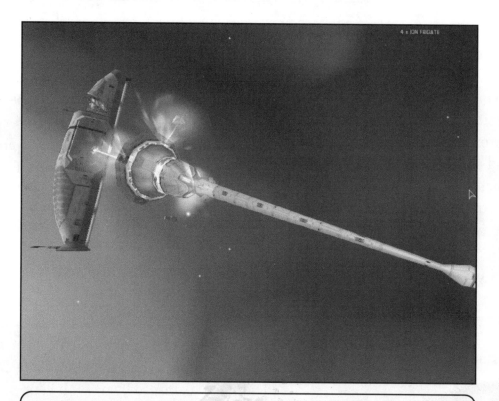

4 x ION FRIGATE

Fig. 5-4. The first two Needle Motherships make a beeline for your own Mothership as soon as you attack them. So hit them hard with your full Battle Group.

After your Battle Group opens fire on the Needle Mothership, the big "inhibitor" slowly lumbers to attack your own Mothership. Lay into her hard with your entire ion gun arsenal. After you finally destroy her, head straight for a second one. (Find it on the Sensors Manager map. It's a yellow ping with a vertical line.) Use the same tactics to destroy her, too.

TIP

Refuel all escort Fighters and Corvettes before you send the Battle Group after the final Needle Mothership, which is more than 100 kilometers away. Your Strike craft are most likely running on fumes by now.

After the second Needle Mothership is space scrap, Fleet Intelligence reports that enemy ships (including the third Needle Mothership) are withdrawing to a point on the map. Send your Battle Group there now. On the way, say "space scrap" really fast 10 times and swat down the pitiful batches of Swarmers and Fuel Pods that try to thwart your advance. Then watch for a group of five Multi–Beam Frigates in Broad formation. Your approach triggers their last-ditch raid. Don't miss them! They fire at your Battle Group, but if you don't kill or capture all five now they continue on toward your lightly defended Mothership.

> **TIP**
>
> Hit [Home] occasionally to check the status of your Mothership and Research Ship (if it's still alive). If stray Swarmers rear their ugly little heads, target their Fuel Pods with your Defense Group.

As you approach the final Needle Mothership, Fleet Intelligence reports on the wreckage floating nearby. Metallurgy and structural composition of the ship are an identical match to the Khar-Toba wreckage on Kharak. It's the

Fig. 5-5. Blast this murderer's row of Multi-Beam Frigates as you near the final Needle Mothership.

Khar-Toba's sister ship! So it's true—you do share a common origin with these frightened Garden dwellers. Gee, too bad you have to waste 'em.

As you approach the last Needle Mothership, send in a Fighter wing first. The big round "head" of this final Mothership doubles as a battering ram, and it tries to turn and ram any attackers. One hit will obliterate any ship in the Mothership's path, no matter how large. Thus, an attack pass by your agile Fighters can draw attention away from your Battle Group—for a while, anyway.

Keep your Capital Ships well away from the Needle Mothership and focus on eliminating all other enemy craft. When that's done and the Needle Mothership is left alone, knock her out with nimble Strike craft attacking in Sphere formation. This way you don't jeopardize your big boats. But be ever vigilant! The Mothership will aggressively seek to ram any Capital Ships she can find.

Once again, don't simply hop to hyperspace as soon as the inhibitor field is finally down. Harvest! Yes, it requires patience. But this nebula is pocked with delicious gas clouds and such. In *Homeworld,* you should always milk as many resources as you can from each region before jumping to the next mission.

Mission 09: Deep Space— "Sea of Lost Souls"

This is a fun little mission. With the proper strategy, it can be a real breather after the wild intensity of the Gardens of Kadesh. But take the wrong approach and you face a brutal exchange—get this—*with your own Capital Ships!* That's right; you can end up battling your own fleet in this diabolically designed scenario if you don't play smart.

Mission Objectives

- Investigate the anomaly.
- Destroy the unknown vessel (the "ghost ship").
- Salvage the unknown vessel.

Research

This mission offers a wealth of technology rewards. When you successfully complete the mission objectives, you salvage Gravity Generator technology from the ghost ship. And if you disabled the ghost ship without destroying the Missile Destroyer in its "escort fleet," you gain Guided Missile technology as a bonus. After that, the Bentusi arrive and offer a trade for Super–Heavy Chassis technology. Nice haul, eh?

Fleet Construction

Your Capital Ships can't get in range of the ghost ship, so your Strike craft bear the burden of finishing the job. Build a strong wing of 20 Attack Bombers to go with the Defenders you already have. You may lose a bunch of these to the ghost ship's "escort fleet," but it's well worth the effort.

Consider building a small group (10 or so) of Scouts for decoy purposes, as well. (See the following Mission Strategy section for details.)

You may need to build a new Salvage Corvette if your previous ones were destroyed in the Cathedral of Kadesh (likely). After that, you can finally start producing the big boys seriously.

Mission Strategy

Your hyperspace jump lands you in a safe area, finally. But Fleet Command reports an anomaly on the sensors and recommends you investigate. Go ahead—send a Probe or Scout to the location.

You discover a massive alien "ghost ship," seemingly long abandoned but surrounded by a motley "escort" of two Multi–Beam Frigates, an Assault Frigate, an Ion Array Frigate, and a new class of Capital Ship—a Missile Destroyer. These vessels are prisoners of a strange "control field" extending about 10 kilometers around the ghost ship that mysteriously seizes all ships in that sphere, directing them to protect the alien vessel.

Fig. 5-6. The zombie escorts are bad enough, but if your Capital Ships get within 10 kilometers of the big ghost ship, it seizes control and turns them against you!

Important: *send no Capital Ships to the anomaly!* Its escort fleet attacks any of your ships that get within about 15 kilometers of the ghost ship. But far worse, its control field seizes command of any of your Capital Ships that get within *10* kilometers of the ghost ship, and then turns them against you. Bummer!

NOTE

You can't destroy the ghost ship. Honest. You can pound on it for hours—nothing. It sports one heck of a super-alien shield.

First, order your Resource Controller to guard your Collector(s) and start harvesting immediately. Next, build two wings of Fighters—20 Attack Bombers in one group and 10 Scouts in the other. Yes, *Scouts.* Now move all Strike craft groups to a position about 17 kilometers from the ghost ship.

Here's the simple plan. Set the Scout group to Evasive Tactics and deploy them out to one side of the ghost ship. This decoy maneuver draws the attention of the escort fleet, the Missile Destroyer in particular. When the coast is clear, send in your other Strike Groups (Defenders and Attack Bombers) to attack the ghost ship from the other side.

Important: Don't attack the Missile Destroyer! Yes, its volleys are lethal to your Strike craft. But the big missile boat joins your fleet as soon as you neutralize the alien control field. When this happens, you gain Guided Missile technology automatically, giving you the ability to build your own Missile Destroyers. On the other hand, if you destroy the Missile Destroyer now, you won't acquire Guided Missile technology until Mission 12.

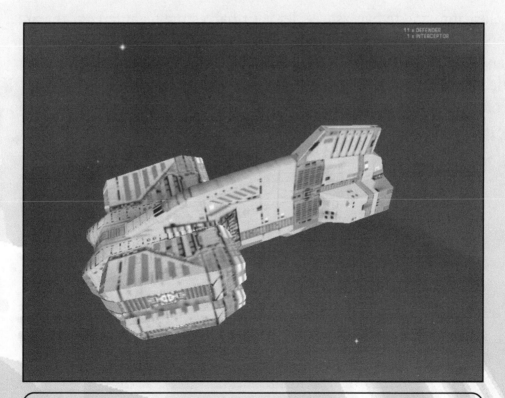

Fig. 5-7. Don't kill this Missile Destroyer! If it survives, it joins your fleet when you disable the ghost ship's control field. Plus, you gain Guided Missile technology.

After you take down the ghost ship's control field, order a Salvage Corvette to "salvage" (explore) the alien craft. Your salvage team learns the vessel is millions of years old, purpose unclear. However, your Research Division uses the alien control field to develop plans for a gravity-warping technology. Begin researching Gravity Generator.

Now the Bentusi arrive. They want the information you acquired from the alien ship and are willing to trade Super–Heavy Chassis technology for it. Hey, that's a done deal. This tech is required for the most massive Capital Ships—Heavy Cruisers and Carriers. In fact, you can build a Carrier right away, if you wish. (You still need Heavy Gun technology to build a Heavy Cruiser.)

After you accept the trade, Fleet Command asks for help against the Taiidan. The Bentusi don't like conflict, but they promise to bring your cause before the Galactic Council—whatever that is.

Before jumping to hyperspace, let your harvesting team tap out the area. A few loads exist, but the resources are spread wide and far, so you must be patient again. Just remember, every load counts. In the meantime, beef up your Battle Group with at least three Destroyers and another Missile Destroyer. If you harvested the Great Nebula fully in the two previous missions, you should have plenty of spare RUs.

CHAPTER 6
THE INNER RIM MISSIONS

As you hop ever closer to Hiigara, your fleet penetrates the outer boundary of the brutal Taiidan empire. This inner-rim region of the galaxy is heavily patrolled, but there are weaknesses you can (and must) exploit. These three missions pit you against increasingly powerful forces, including your first confrontation with the Taiidan Heavy Cruiser.

MISSION 10: SUPER NOVA RESEARCH STATION

The Taiidan imperial forces are formidable, but Fleet Intelligence has identified a weak point in the enemy's defensive sphere—a remote Research Station near an active supernova. Because of the intense radiation in the area, you can expect lighter-than-normal resistance.

This intense radiation poses its own problems, however. Strike craft burn up quickly, and even Capital Ships suffer gradual damage from exposure to the supernova's debilitating rays. But Fleet Intelligence has learned that veins of space dust in the area have shielding properties.

You can bet the enemy knows this, too. Do you suppose the Taiidan have strung up "Welcome" banners along these shielded dust paths to their research outpost?

Mission Objectives

- Destroy the research outpost.

Research

- Proximity Sensor
- Minelaying Tech

Fleet Construction

Forget your Strike craft. The supernova radiation will fry anything smaller than a Frigate—even in the shielded veins of space dust. Plus, some real heavyweights lurk near the research outpost, including a Taiidan Heavy Cruiser. You'd better pump out a few big boys of your own.

To attempt the Strong Fleet option discussed in the Mission Strategy section, you'll need a Battle Group with at least three Destroyers and two Missile Destroyers, and a healthy contingent of Ion Cannon Frigates—10 or more, if possible. The Missile Destroyers are particularly good against the Strike craft swarms and minefields you'll encounter on the central path to the Research Station. If you don't have *at least* one Missile Destroyer in your attack group, opt for the Midsized Fleet option.

Fig. 6-1. Include at least two Missile Destroyers in your attack group, or these Taiidan Minelayer Corvettes will make your trek to the Research Station a painful one.

Enemy Deployment

In this mission, you may choose from several routes to the target, each with a different deployment of enemy ships. The enemy fleet arrayed near the supernova station includes:

A Carrier

A Heavy Cruiser

Two Destroyers

Four Ion Cannon Frigates

12 Assault Frigates

14 Multigun Corvettes

45 Defenders

Two Minelayer Corvettes
(and several minefields)

Eight Heavy Corvettes

13 Attack Bombers

13 Interceptors

You also must contend with radiation damage from the supernova, which limits ship movement to the asteroid paths (except for short trips between paths).

Most ships are deployed in two areas. The Taiidan's primary defense force guards the central dust vein—Minelayers and their minefields, Interceptors, Heavy Corvettes, Destroyers and the Heavy Cruiser—and the Research Station—Carrier, Attack Bombers, Multigun Corvettes, Ion Cannon Frigates, and two of the Assault Frigates. The other Assault Frigates are deployed in two groups of five along the outer dust paths.

After your forces destroy the station, all surviving Taiidan ships on the map will move toward your attack group.

Mission Strategy

The two strategies for this mission come courtesy of Christopher Mason of the Sierra *Homeworld* Quality Assurance team. The strategy you choose depends on whether you currently have a Strong or Midsized fleet.

As Mason puts it, "If you come into this mission with a *weak* fleet—well, go back and do Mission 9 again."

Strong Fleet Strategy

A "strong" fleet comprises at least 10 Ion Cannon Frigates (including Ion Array Frigates and/or Multibeam Frigates), at least three Destroyers, and at least one Missile Destroyer—two or three, if possible. (Again, if you have no Missile Destroyer, try the Midsized Fleet strategy.) With this fleet, you can head straight up the central dust path (the one marked by the all those red dots in the Sensors Manager).

Before you do anything else, send your resource collection team out to harvest that thick cluster of asteroids off to the left of your Mothership. (See Figure 6-2.) Your Collectors suffer some radiation damage en route, but once they reach the asteroids, the big rocks shield them as they harvest.

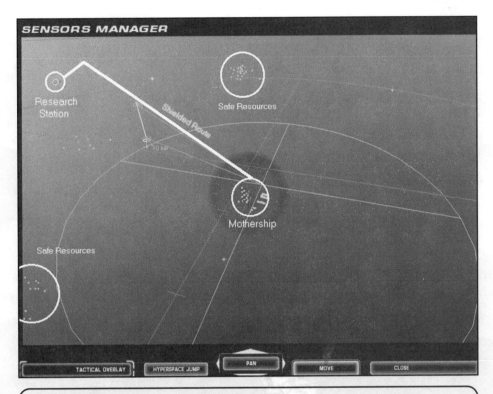

Fig. 6-2. Take the "high road." Follow the dust vein's upward angle through the red dots until you engage the Taiidan Heavy Cruiser group; then descend to the Research Station.

Next, array your Battle Group. Order all your Capital Ships into a single Wall formation. This way, your Missile Destroyers can blast enemy Strike craft and minefields but still receive support from the rest of the group.

It's time to move. Important: *Do not go directly toward the Research Station's yellow ping on the Sensors Manager!* That route runs *below* the

CAUTION

Stay in the dust paths! If your Battle Group tries to make a direct run for the Taiidan Research Station, many of your Frigate-class ships will burn up en route, and you'll arrive with seriously degraded Super Capital Ships, too.

dust vein, leaving your group unshielded. Instead, move the Battle Group forward *and up* to the first red dot. Note that the dust vein runs "uphill" from your starting point through the red dots on the way to the Research Station.

The first red dot turns out to be an 'X' of 12 Interceptors accompanied by seven Heavy Corvettes in front of a wall of mines. Target them immediately; your Missile Destroyers should make short work of them. When the Fighters and Corvettes are dead, move the Battle Group forward and "force attack" the mines ahead; that is, hold down Ctrl + Shift and drag a selection box around the entire minefield.

TIP

Watch carefully for the mines. They're hard to pinpoint because they resemble small space rocks. Look for little red-orange dots in symmetrical formations.

Minesweeping is no picnic. Even with a pair of Missile Destroyers, your Battle Group will miss a number of the mines that swarm and seek your ships (which is why you should use three Missile Destroyers, if you can). Once your fleet fire sweeps the minefield clean, move the entire group forward again. Soon you hit

Fig. 6-3. Missile Destroyers help pave the way through Fighters and mine-infested dust veins.

another minefield, this one surrounding the dastardly Minelaying Corvette responsible for all the nasty little floaters. Again, force attack the mines to clear the way.

Continue this force attack tactic to clear several more minefields and another Minelaying Corvette on the upward path along the dust vein. Keep working from red dot to red dot on the Sensors Manager. As your fleet nears the Research Station, a Heavy Cruiser and two Destroyers rear their ugly heads. Destroy them!

CAUTION

Monitor your harvester activity! Collectors should harvest only the two larger asteroid fields nearest your Mothership— the one to the left first, and then the one to the right. If you forget about your harvesters, they may wander forward to the smaller asteroid fields and run into groups of enemy Assault Frigates.

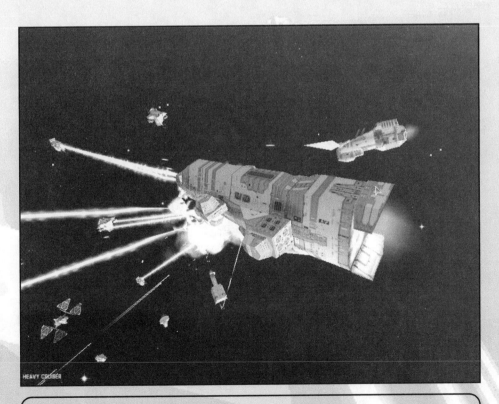

Fig. 6-4. Meet your first Heavy Cruiser with a friendly dose of concentrated fire. Ignore its companion Destroyers until you kill it.

Now it's downhill (literally), about 40 kilometers to the research outpost. Of course, it isn't unprotected. When you reach the station, direct your full Battle Group to attack the Taiidan Carrier; if it gets away, you lose! As the ion cannons roar, select your Missile Destroyers individually and order them to attack the enemy Strike craft harassing your Battle Group. The moment the Carrier blows, turn your Battle Group's attention to the enemy Frigates hovering near the station—but keep your Missile Destroyers hitting the enemy Strike craft. Wipe out the entire defense force, down to the last Fighter.

Fig. 6-5. Save the Research Station for last. It has no guns and can't hurt you.

Finally, lay into the Research Station itself with everything you've got. As you do, keep your eye out for the two groups of five Assault Frigates returning from guard duty in the dust paths. After you destroy the station and any returning Frigates, let your Battle Group hang while you direct your harvesting efforts. As always, suck the region dry of resources before you go. Then build a few more Super Capital Ships for your Battle Group. In fact, if you can, max out the number of Destroyers and Missile Destroyers you own.

Midsized Fleet Strategy

This is definitely Plan B.

Your first goal should be to build a strong force to face the perils that lie ahead. But if your fleet just isn't strong enough to face the Heavy Cruiser/ Destroyers, or if you have no Missile Destroyers to deal with the mines, and you don't want to replay earlier missions to create a bigger fleet, you can still win this mission.

How? Remember, other dust veins lead to the Research Station. These side paths aren't well-guarded. (Indeed, you can avoid even the two Assault Frigate groups.) However, these routes are less direct and harder to navigate, requiring you to leave the dust veins to change paths, taking radiation damage in the process. Still, with patience and care, you can get your fleet to the Research Station intact. Once there, use the same order of attack as for the Strong Fleet approach—Carrier first, then Frigates, Strike craft, and finally the station itself.

MISSION II: TENHAUSER GATE

An intercepted Taiidan transmission confirms your race's ancient, almost mythical status as "the Exiles." The decrypted message also reveals that the Taiidan are seriously ticked off at the Bentusi for seeking to bring the matter of your return before the Council. As you arrive at Tenhauser Gate, eight Taiidan Capital Ships are trying to put a few ion beams up the ol' Bentusi tailpipe.

Mission Objectives

- Destroy the Taiidan fleet.

Research

No new technology this mission.

Fleet Construction

If most of your fleet survived Mission 10, you should be in good shape without adding many new ships. Three small groups of Scouts can draw Taiidan fire from the Bentusi vessel quickly. Then, of course, you need a stout Battle Group—10 to 12 Ion Cannon Frigates, three to five Destroyers, two or three Missile Destroyers—to eliminate the eight Taiidan Capital Ships efficiently. If you try the "bonus move" (described later), you'd better have six to eight Salvage Corvettes. It takes four to drag in a Heavy Cruiser, and you're sure to lose a few during the attempt.

Mission Strategy

Here's a good, old-fashioned, slug-it-out sort of mission. Enemies confronting you—one Heavy Cruiser, three Destroyers, four Ion Cannon Frigates, all grouped by class, all attacking the Bentusi as the scenario begins.

Your first goal is to draw all Taiidan fire away from the traders' Mothership. Easy enough. When you shoot any ship in one of the class groups, *all* the ships in that group will stop attacking the Bentusi and attack you. In other words, if you attack one Taiidan Frigate, it and all three of its sister Frigates will turn from the Bentusi to meet your challenge.

So attack three Taiidan ships *immediately*—one Destroyer, one Ion Cannon Frigate, and the Heavy Cruiser. Send small groups of Scouts or Interceptors to get there quickly as you put your primary Battle Group in Wall formation. Even the pecking fire of a single Scout will draw the full attention of each class of ship. Of course, now *you're* under the gun. But that's the price you pay for being a hero.

The rest of the battle is straightforward. When your Battle Group finally lumbers into range, concentrate its fire on each Taiidan ship, from biggest to

Fig. 6-6. The key to this mission is to draw Taiidan fire from the Bentusi ASAP. Send speedy Strike craft to attack a Frigate, a Destroyer, and the Heavy Cruiser.

smallest—Heavy Cruiser first, then Destroyers, then Frigates. Or, if you're very skilled with your Salvage Corvettes, you can try to grab the Heavy Cruiser—a juicy prize, indeed. It takes five Salvage Corvettes to capture one, and its swiveling guns make it hard to approach from *any* direction. But it might be worth the effort.

Bonus Move

To nab the Heavy Cruiser, focus your Battle Group's concentrated fire on the Destroyers and Frigates while you harass the Cruiser with swarms of Strike craft. When only the Cruiser remains, slip two groups of five to six Salvage Corvettes behind it, and then try the grab. You'll probably lose Corvettes in the attempt, but chances are good that four of the eight will latch on.

After you rescue the Bentusi, they repay you with the best currency known to man—self-knowledge. In the wars of the "First Time," the vicious Taiidan exiled your ancestors from your homeworld. The Guidestone, you learn, is the only artifact of your true legacy that survived the perilous odyssey. But the Bentusi note how many cultures have prophesied your return.

In the First Time, a terrible war brought with it the collapse of your ancient empire. So vicious were your enemies that all would have been slaughtered were it not for the collective outcry for mercy.

Fig. 6-7. In gratitude for the rescue, the Bentusi show you the Big Picture.

Their final words: "Reach your homeworld. Establish your claim. We will summon the Council."

Now your Resource Collectors can harvest all resources in the area. Meanwhile, open your Launch Manager and click the Remain Docked button under the Mothership icon. (You'll learn why in a minute.) When the area is harvested down to pebbles, jump to hyperspace.

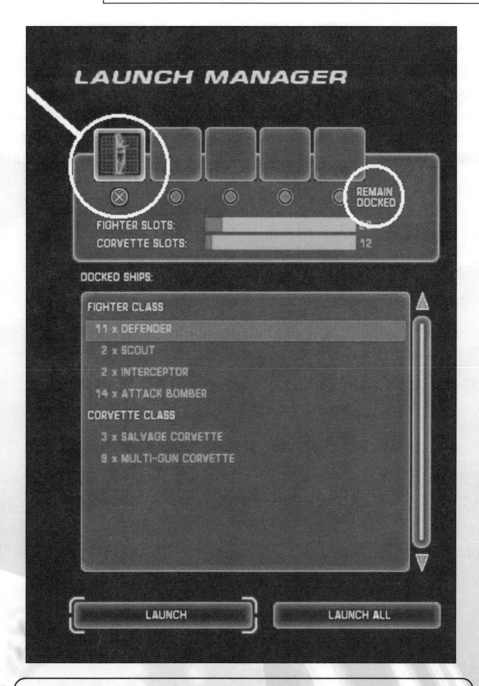

Fig. 6-8. Click the Remain Docked button in the Launch Manager **before** you make your hyperspace jump. You want all Strike craft to remain inside the Mothership as Mission 12 begins.

MISSION 12: GALACTIC CORE

The Bentusi have revealed your origins. Now a mysterious quantum waveform collapse drops you into the lap of Taiidan vengeance. Grav Well Generators pull you from hyperspace and threaten to make sitting ducks of any Strike craft you launch. Plus, your enemy introduces a sneaky new technology: cloaked Taiidan ships make life hell until you counter with Proximity Sensors. But at mission's end, aid comes to your exiled race from an unexpected source.

Mission Objectives

- Protect the fleet.
- Destroy the source of the gravity field.
- Protect the defector.

Research

- Cloaked Fighter

Fleet Construction

The Taiidan try to sneak some cloaked ships at you. Counter with Proximity Sensors! They're cheap but vulnerable, so build a bunch; five or six is good. You face many waves of enemy Strike craft, so be sure you have at least two Missile Destroyers in your Battle Group. Don't stock up on your own Strike craft, though. Enemy Grav Well Generators will render them useless.

Fig. 6-9. Man's best friend against cloaked ships is a Proximity Sensor. Order two to guard each fleet group.

Mission Strategy

Yes, another trap! You emerge from hyperspace surrounded by three Grav Well Generators (each with two Support Frigates), which will immobilize any Strike craft you launch. Then two Taiidan Assault Frigates and a Missile Destroyer pounce on your frozen little ships. Of course, if you took our advice at the end of Mission 11 and clicked the Remain Docked button in the Launch Manager *before* your hyperspace jump, your Strike craft are nestled safely in the womb of your Mothership.

Whatever the case, your Battle Group should make short work of the enemy's opening gambit. But two Taiidan Carrier groups and a small Taiidan Battle Group with a full escort of support ships lurk out there in the asteroids

Fig. 6-10. If you (foolishly) launched Strike craft, you'd better kill these Grav Well Generators right away.

and dust clouds. Soon the Carriers launch waves of Fighters and Corvettes at you. Important: *Stay at home!* If you chase stragglers or hunt the Carrier groups, you can run into deadly minefields and, worse, engage in unnecessary combat.

TIP

Build Proximity Sensors immediately! Sierra tester Chris Mason says, "Generally, I order at least two to guard each of my major groups. That way, whichever group encounters cloaked ships, they can deal with it." One other tip—once you locate an enemy Cloak Generator, kill it **before** you target the cloaked ship(s).

Early waves feature wings of Scouts; Interceptors; Attack Bombers; a few Heavy Corvettes; various combinations of the foregoing ships; a deadly trio of Minelayer Corvettes (who lay a wall of mines, and then try to lure you there), and a cloaked Ion Cannon Frigate with a Cloak Generator. If you have your full allotment of three Missile Destroyers and a few Proximity Sensors, none of these waves should present major trouble. Again, the key—stay at home!

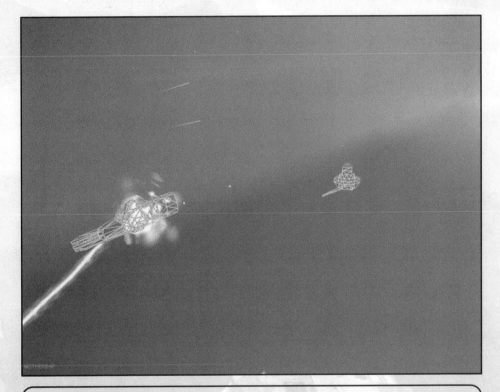

Fig. 6-11. Your Proximity Sensors reveal cloaked ships in "wireframe" outline. Here, you see a Taiidan Ion Cannon Frigate and its Cloak Generator.

CAUTION

Enemy ships accompanied by a Cloak Generator will target your Proximity Sensors. Keep several Proximity Sensors in each of your groups, and hold some in reserve near the Mothership for backup.

Eventually, the main attack begins—a Taiidan Heavy Cruiser with an escort of 20 Defenders, five Heavy Corvettes, and four Ion Frigates. This is no trifling assault, but your full Battle Group should handle it expeditiously. As always, focus on the big ship first, although you can split off your Missile Destroyers to pop all those annoying Strike craft.

As soon as you've destroyed the Taiidan Cruiser, a defector named Captain Elson suddenly hyperspaces in:

"Attention Kushan Mothership! This is Captain Elson of the Taiidan Elite Guard Destroyer *Kapella*. We wish to defect and need assistance. In return we are prepared to help you. Please respond."

Fig. 6-12. Hustle to rescue Captain Elson's Elite Guard Destroyer. If he dies, you lose.

Bring up your Sensors Manager to view his position. Captain Elson's badly wounded Destroyer (the yellow ping) is speeding toward your Mothership from the front-left, pursued by eight Interceptors (with a Support Frigate), two Assault Frigates, and two Ion Frigates. Polish off any remaining escorts of the now-dead Heavy Cruiser with your Battle Group, but split off a contingent to hustle toward Elson's Destroyer. You can launch a few of the Strike craft docked in your Mothership to help Elson, as well.

Once the defector is safely aboard the Mothership and you get the go-ahead to make a hyperspace jump, do it! In previous missions, you've hung around to harvest an area dry. And a glance at your Sensors Manager reveals plentiful resources being harvested by Taiidan collectors. So you'll be tempted to run out and compete for rocks.

Fight that temptation this time. The Taiidan Carriers pose no threat unless you go looking for trouble. And Minelayer Corvettes spitting out minefields will cost you more than you're likely to gain in a fight for the area's resources.

CHAPTER 7
THE HIIGARA MISSIONS

This final quartet of missions takes you from a junkyard in the hinterlands of the Hiigara system to the shimmering planet itself—your birthright, your homeworld. On the way you sneak (or hack) through a Taiidan defense that includes Field Generators to knock you out of hyperspace and a massive, deadly "object" that threatens to transform your Mothership into an entirely different quantum waveform known as "smithereens."

MISSION 13:
THE KAROS GRAVEYARD—
"THE SHINING HINTERLANDS"

Group Captain Elson belongs to the Rebellion, a resistance corps that despises the decadent and corrupt imperial government. He says the Taiidan fleet's incineration of Kharak's atmosphere has become the final catalyst for an uprising. So now you have other guys on your side.

Captain Elson wants to contact his group via a hidden Communications Relay Station in the midst of a ship graveyard. Your sole objective is to dock a Strike craft (Fighter or Corvette) with the Relay Station to establish a link. Elson believes he can find a way through the Taiidan defenses surrounding your homeworld, and thus "help the Rebellion move into its next phase."

Mission Objectives

- Dock the Strike craft with the Communications Relay.

Research

- Heavy Guns (at last!)
- Cloak Generator

Fleet Construction

For this mission you need only a handful of Strike craft and a couple of Missile Destroyers.

Mission Strategy

The Karos ship graveyard is pretty spooky and presents some serious challenges. Dozens of Autoguns—small, self-contained, automated firing systems—litter the yard. These guns are immobile, but quite deadly. And although you'll soon have both Cloaked Fighter and Cloak Generator technology, the junkyard's numerous Proximity Sensors complicate the cloaking option.

The worse menace is the Junkyard Dog, a nearly indestructible ship snatcher that makes the average Salvage Corvette seem like a Tonka toy. This vicious robotic vessel is programmed to target any Capital Ship that wanders into Karos and haul off trespassers to the various hyperspace gates scattered throughout the junkyard. Once any ship—even a Destroyer—is in the Dog's grasp, there's no escape.

Thus, any direct push through the graveyard will cost you some ships. But the Autoguns and Junkyard Dog both have upper and lower limits to their range. To sneak through virtually undetected, create a contact group of Missile Destroyers and a strong wing of Strike craft (any kind will do). In the Sensors Manager, send this group *vertically* straight up to the top (or straight down to the bottom) of the map. Then move it horizontally until it's directly above (or

Fig. 7-1. This Dog rules the junkyard. If you let him sneak up on your Capital Ships (such as this unfortunate Frigate), he'll haul them off to a hyperspace gate.

below) the Relay Station (the yellow ping on your Sensors Manager map). Order the Strike craft group to guard your Missile Destroyers; you want the big boats in front when you finally descend (or ascend) to the station.

Keep an eye on the Junkyard Dog, the only moving red dot on your Sensors Manager. When it wanders to the front of the yard (the fringe nearest your Mothership), send your contact group straight down (or up) to the Relay Station. As you approach, a vicious pack of Autoguns will open fire. Take them out with your Missile Destroyers. Then select your Strike craft group and click on the Relay Station. One of your Fighters or Corvettes will dock and establish the communications link.

Fig. 7-2. Select your Strike craft and click on this Relay Station to dock.

After you establish the communications link, jump to hyperspace and use the Quick Docking option to get your Missile Destroyers out of the junkyard before the Dog bites.

TIP

Even if you use the foregoing strategy, the Junkyard Dog still may sneak up on a Missile Destroyer in your contact group. To minimize this possibility, build a cheap Frigate—the Support Frigate costs only 425 RUs—and send it to the forward fringe of the junkyard. (Try to park in a place Autoguns can't reach.) Immediately, the Dog will move forward to grab your sacrificial lamb. Wait until it gets close, and then send your contact group down to the Relay Station. The Dog can't get back before you establish your link for Captain Elson.

MISSION 14: BRIDGE OF SIGHS

An array of massive Field Generators maintains a network of inhibitor fields that blocks hyperspace access to Hiigara's system. But Captain Elson's Rebel contacts have identified the most vulnerable Field Generator; if you can destroy it, you can create your own access point for jumping to the brink of your homeworld. Unfortunately, dozens of Taiidan Ion Cannon Frigates and hundreds of Strike craft form a huge defensive sphere around your target.

Mission Objectives

Primary

- Destroy the field generator.

Secondary

- Destroy the hyperspace gates.

> **NOTE**
>
> Sensors Array is the last technology available in **Homeworld**'s single-player game.

Research

- Sensors Array

Fleet Construction

Refer to both strategies in the following section. Each requires a different fleet configuration.

Mission Strategy

The trick here is to slip through a teeming sphere of Taiidan vessels with a Battle Group big enough to take out the eight massive components of the Field Generator. Then you can jump to hyperspace (using Quick Docking) before the rest of the defense sphere descends.

No problem! The Sierra *Homeworld* testers have developed a couple of good ways to go about this task.

The Sneak Attack

You'll need six Cloak Generators, six Heavy Cruisers and/or Destroyers, and 15–20 Attack Bombers.

This elegant strategy has you sneak a small but powerful Battle Group right into the heart of the Taiidan defensive sphere without being detected—until you open fire on the Field Generator. The key to this approach is the way you group your Cloak Generators and then position your attack fleet within their cloaking field.

Group the six Cloak Generators this way: First, create two groups of three generators and number them Group 1 and Group 2. Then create three more groups, each comprising one generator from Group 1 and one from Group 2. To be painfully explicit, Group 3 should include the first Cloak Generator from Group 1 and the first from Group 2. Group 4 includes the second generator from Group 1 and the second from Group 2. Group 5 includes the third generator from Group 1 and the third from Group 2.

Got it?

Hang in there. It's less complicated than it seems. This arrangement allows you to position Groups 1 and 2 (the groups of three) at either end of your attack group of Cruisers, Destroyers, and Attack Bombers, keeping all ships within a cloaking field. Then you can use Groups 3, 4, and 5 (the pairs) to turn specific pairs of generators on or off—one each from the "positioning" groups 1 and 2.

Fig. 7-3. Six Super Capital Ships, a handful of Attack Bombers, and three pairs of Cloak Generators can win this mission. Be sure the cloaking fields cover the entire group.

Now take the following steps:

1. Put the Heavy Cruisers and Destroyers—again, a total of six in any combination—into Wall formation and designate them Group 6.
2. Put the Attack Bombers in Broad formation and order the group to guard the lower Super Capital Ship in the middle of the Wall formation.
3. Put groups 1 and 2 (the groups of three Cloak Generators) each into Broad formation.
4. Order Group 1 to guard the lower-right Super Capital Ship.
5. Order Group 2 to guard the lower-left Super Capital Ship.

Now run a test with the Cloak Generator pairs in groups 3, 4, and 5 to verify that *all* ships in the small fleet are within the cloaking fields of each pair of generators. Here's how:

1. Press ③ to select the Group 3 pair of Cloak Generators, and then press ⓩ to cloak. Make sure all ships are cloaked.
2. Order Group 6 (your Cruisers and Destroyers) to move forward a short distance.
3. If any ships become uncloaked during the move, reposition the fleet to create a tighter formation. If the entire wing of Attack Bombers doesn't fit in the cloaking field, consider peeling off the visible Bombers.
4. When all ships are cloaked, press ③, and then ⓩ again to decloak.
5. Repeat the foregoing steps to test the cloaking fields of the Cloak Generator pairs in groups 4 and 5.
6. If you made adjustments in Step 5, double-check the cloaking fields of previously tested Cloak Generator pairs.

Order Group 6 (your Super Capital Ships) to head toward the Taiidan Field Generator (the yellow ping at the center of the red-dotted sphere in your Sensors Manager). When you get about halfway to the outer edge of the sphere of enemy ships, turn on one pair of Cloak Generators. As you progress toward the Field Generator, keep an eye on the brown power bars of your active pair of Cloak Generators. When they're about to run out of cloak juice, switch on another pair.

By alternating three pairs of Cloak Generators, you can stay cloaked indefinitely. Once you get to the Taiidan Field Generator, destroy it (all eight sections in the ring)—and then get the heck out of there (hyperspace immediately and use Quick Docking).

Fig. 7-4. The Field Generator is arrayed in eight sections. You must destroy them all before you can hyperspace away.

The Capture Ploy

You'll need three Cloak Generators, two to six Salvage Corvettes, and a large Battle Group.

This strategy is similar to the previous one. Instead of cloaking your attack fleet to sneak to the Field Generator, however, you'll cloak Salvage Corvettes to "steal" a

TIP

About the Mission 14 secondary objective—don't bother to destroy the hyperspace gates. If you use either of these two mission strategies, you won't be around to face enemy reinforcements.

hole in the defensive sphere (and simultaneously reinforce your fleet). Basically, you use three Cloak Generators to maintain a continuous cloaking field for the Salvage Corvettes, who then sneak into the enemy sphere and capture ships.

This is a fun way to open a path through the Taiidan defense for your Battle Group. As a bonus, you increase your fleet size by stealing enemy Frigates. The downside: this is *very* time-consuming and sometimes enemy ships follow your Salvage Corvettes (which must decloak while salvaging) back to your Mothership. If this happens, use your main fleet to kick some Taiidan butt, and then recloak those Salvage Corvettes as soon as they drop off their booty.

TIP

If your Battle Group doesn't have at least 10 Ion Cannon Frigates by now, use the Capture Ploy to beef up your fleet. It may take a long time, but your patience will be rewarded in the final **Homeworld** missions.

NOTE

A third strategy simply combines these two. Use cloaked Salvage Corvettes to steal enemy Ion Cannon Frigates to add firepower to your fleet. Then create and send in a cloaked attack group to eliminate the Field Generator with minimal losses.

MISSION 15: CHAPEL PERILOUS

Yes, the fleet is ready. There can be no retreat now. But your jump to the Hiigara system has been interrupted. Your fleet drops out of hyperspace into the path of a very, very large object. If it hits your Mothership—good-bye.

Mission Objectives

- Destroy the object (the "Rockship").

Fleet Construction

You'll have very little time to build anything once this mission starts. You should drop into the mission with a strong Battle Group that includes Heavy Cruisers, a full allotment of Destroyers, and at least 10 Ion Cannon Frigates.

Mission Strategy

It's simple: go kill the Rockship. And hurry! *But stay out of its way.* Like the final Needle Mothership in the Cathedral of Kadesh, this massive vessel will plow through a Frigate, a Destroyer, or even a Heavy Cruiser like a fist through gelatin.

Fig. 7-5. Lock onto the Rockship with your Heavy Cruisers and Ion Cannon Frigates. But be careful! Here it plows happily through the Cruiser at the upper left.

Also, you must preserve as much of your fleet as you can for the final mission. So dispose of the Rockship's escort units while you hit the Rockship. (You don't want them shooting up your tailpipe as you chase the Rockship.) One suggestion: split your Battle Group. Send Heavy Cruisers and Ion Cannon Frigates after the Rockship. Direct Destroyers (including Missile Destroyers) to focus on the Capital Ships in the enemy escort group. Group-attack the waves of enemy Strike craft with any available Interceptors, Defenders, and/or Multigun Corvettes.

After the Rockship explodes, harvest the area. Build one Support Frigate and at least two Repair Corvettes for the next mission. Then spend all remaining RUs to create a good fleet balance between Capital Ships and Strike craft. Ideally, you should go into the final Homeworld mission with two or three Heavy Cruisers, five Destroyers, three Missile Destroyers, 10 or more Ion Cannon Frigates (or the equivalent), and wings of 15–20 Attack Bombers, 10–12 Multigun Corvettes, 15–20 Interceptors, and a few Defenders, as well.

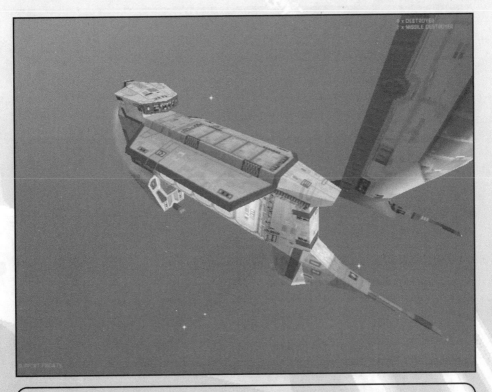

Fig. 7-6. Build at least one Support Frigate for the final mission.

> **TIP**
>
> Retire all harvesters (except one Resource Collector and one Resource Controller), all Proximity Sensors and Sensors Arrays, and all Cloak Generators. Convert the RUs from these into warships of your choice.

MISSION 16: HIIGARA

And here you are. Hiigara, finally. Look at that blue planet with its single Angel Moon satellite. Seems a tad more hospitable than Kharak—well, once you get past those bloodthirsty Taiidan fleets, anyway. And speaking of that, get ready for some seriously intense combat. This final mission features four very difficult battles, including a classic split-fleet confrontation with superior forces.

Want your homeworld back? Earn it.

Fig. 7-7. Hiigara, your homeworld, at last! Say, doesn't this place look sort of...familiar?

Mission Objectives

- Eradicate enemy forces.

Fleet Construction

Don't hold back here. This mission is a Capital Ship slugathon. When your Resource Collector dumps loads of RUs, build big boats to replace those you lose. Even with the full allotment of three Heavy Cruisers, five Destroyers, three Missile Destroyers, and 20 Frigates (15 Ion Cannon for combat, five Support to keep the Mothership alive), the action in Hiigara's shadow is relentless, furious, and draining.

A Note about "Chugging" Frame Rates

A *lot* of units fly around in this mission, severely taxing your system resources. All but the most powerful machines probably will experience some "chugging"—slow frame rates that can render game action (and your cursor movement) a little jerky. This can make it tough to micromanage so many ships.

To overcome chugging, simply *pause the game*—and do it frequently. Pause whenever you're selecting or grouping ships. And, although you can't issue attack orders with the game paused, you can set them up. When you're ready to issue a new attack order, pause the game and select the ships you want to order. Then hold down [Alt] and click on the target for a close-up. Finally, unpause the game and quickly issue the attack command.

This technique eliminates the frustration of repeatedly trying to click on a moving target and missing it because of the "chug" effect. The [Alt]-Focus command keeps the camera focused on the target—that is, keeps the target in the center of the screen. So when you unpause the game to order the attack, you can't miss.

Mission Strategy

You fight four titanic battles in this mission. None is easy, so *save often*, particularly in the lulls between battles.

Hiigara: Battle One

Three forces advance on your Mothership as the mission opens—a group of five Ion Cannon Frigates from below, wings of Heavy Corvettes and Attack Bombers launched by a Carrier from above, and—the main threat—a major Battle Group from in front. Here's an effective way to deploy your forces.

First, *immediately* send your Resource Controller/Collector(s) team out to harvest. The sooner you start collecting RUs, the better. Plus, this move gets your harvesters out of harm's way.

Second, send a Missile Destroyer and/or any Strike craft that aren't great against Capital Ships (Interceptors, Multigun Corvettes) up to the enemy Carrier. Focus on the launched enemy Strike craft; don't worry about killing the Carrier itself. It won't bother you once its Strike Craft are dead.

Third, send a few Ion Cannon Frigates, with any Strike craft that *are* good against Capital Ships (Attack Bombers, Heavy Corvettes), down to take out the five enemy Ion Cannon Frigates. Try to knock them out before they reach your Mothership, because this series of battles throws a lot of fire at it.

Fourth, group your Support Frigates and order them to repair the Mothership. The more of these you have sucking away the pain, the better.

Fig. 7-8. Put five or six Support Frigates to work repairing your Mothership the minute it takes its first damage.

Now confront the main threat with your own Battle Group. This first Taiidan fleet, in order of threat to your Mothership, includes a Heavy Cruiser, five Ion Cannon Frigates, two Destroyers, two Missile Destroyers, and five Assault Frigates. Attack them in that order, concentrating your fire for quick kills.

If you win, save your game! You should have time to repair your Mothership and any severely damaged Capital Ships, using the Support Frigates. Meanwhile, split your Battle Group into two roughly equal units. Place one in front of your Mothership, the other behind.

Fig. 7-9. The Taiidan assault waves include some Heavy Cruisers, Destroyers, Missile Destroyers, and multiple Ion Cannon and Assault Frigates.

Hiigara: Battle Two

Soon Fleet Intelligence reports, "Enemy reinforcements emerging from hyperspace." The Taiidan fleet emerges behind and above you. Again, the key is to keep Mothership damage to a minimum, so move your rear-guard fleet halfway up to meet them. This Taiidan group will mix it up, unlike the first one (which ignored your fleet and went straight for the Mothership). So the farther from the Mothership you engage this enemy group, the fewer shots they'll take at it.

Just in case, however, get your Support Frigates working on the Mothership.

This rear assault, in order of your attack, includes a Heavy Cruiser, five Ion Cannon Frigates, three Destroyers, and five pesky Assault Frigates. This is a tough fight with only half your forces. But, again, be disciplined and concentrate fire on one ship at a time.

During this engagement, Fleet Intelligence announces again, "Enemy reinforcements emerging from hyperspace." Uh-oh. The half-fleet you left in front of the Mothership soon will face a wave of Taiidan death that duplicates the first enemy wave back in Battle One—a Heavy Cruiser, five Ion Cannon Frigates, two Destroyers, two Missile Destroyers, and five Assault Frigates.

You know the drill by now. Good luck.

After you win this brutal two-front battle, you may not have much time to repair and rebuild for the next attack. Keep those Support Frigates healing the Mothership. Save the game. And get ready for a surprise.

> **TIP**
>
> When you split your forces, be sure to keep a close eye on both groups. The easiest way to keep tabs is to designate them Group 1 and Group 2. To check back and forth, press P to pause the game, press 1 and then 1 for a close-up of Group 1, and then press 2 and 2 for a close-up of Group 2. Do this frequently during this second battle.

Hiigara: Battle Three

This can be a tough battle if your Mothership is heavily damaged. Maybe you heard, but another Taiidan fleet dropped from hyperspace at the tail end of the previous battle. Now a Heavy Cruiser, nine Ion Cannon Frigates, and nine Assault Frigates sneak up from behind and below you. About the time they arrive, Fleet Intelligence reports yet *another* fleet dropping right on top of you. The slightly panicked voice admits, "We're being overwhelmed!"

But guess what? It's Captain Elson, the defector. And he brings help. Elson attacks the enemy with his Elite Guard Destroyer and some Ion Cannon Frigates. He also gives you command of his Assault Frigates and Missile Destroyers. Cool! Get those into the fray as soon as you can. If your Mothership is fairly healthy, you and the good Captain should finish successfully. Remember to keep repairing the Mothership during the battle and to save when you win.

Hiigara: Battle Four

As soon as your Mothership is safe, Captain Elson takes his ships and heads toward the emperor's Mothership. Follow him with every combat ship you have left. The enemy mounts no more attacks against your Mothership, so throw everything you have at the emperor.

Fig. 7-10. Group Captain Elson, the Taiidan defector, arrives to help clean up the mess around your Mothership. Then he crosses the map to hit this Taiidan Carrier. Stay with him, or he'll lose most of his unit!

Elson's group targets a Taiidan Carrier first. If you don't keep up with him, the Carrier's Strike craft will decimate his unit. Help him if you can: it's nice to keep his Destroyer and Frigates alive for the final siege...because three Taiidan Heavy Cruisers (with two Support Frigates each) defend the emperor's Mothership with fanatical loyalty. As always, concentrate fire on the Cruisers one at a time.

When the Cruisers are toast, hit that Mothership! A pair of listless Taiidan Missile Destroyers hovers nearby, but they don't defend aggressively. Level every gun you have on the emperor's house. Remember, this is an all-or-nothing battle. Even if the emperor's escort wipes out all your ships but a single Scout, you still win as long as you've destroyed his Mothership.

Fig. 7-11. Once you get past the three Taiidan Heavy Cruisers and reach the emperor's Mothership, the game is in your hands.

Congratulations! It was a long haul across the galaxy, but you're finally home. Enjoy the credits and the very cool song by Yes.

INDEX

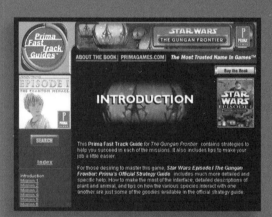